# Long Life
# Good Health

## Through
## Tai-Chi Chuan

盧瀅如編著

太極拳

一九九〇庚午年秋於舊金山唐人埠

# Long Life
# Good Health

## Through
## Tai-Chi Chuan

Simmone Kuo

BLUE SNAKE BOOKS
BERKELEY, CALIFORNIA

ISBN: 1-55643-111-2
ISBN-13: 978-1-55643-111-1

Published by
Blue Snake Books

Blue Snake Books publications are distrubuted by
North Atlantic Books
P.O. Box 12327
Berkeley, California 94712

Cover art by Sy Lin Chu-Sheng and Lin Yi-Hung
Cover and book design by Paula Morrison
Printed in the United States of America

*Long Life, Good Health, Through Tai-Chi Chuan* is sponsored by the Society for the Study of Native Arts and Sciences, a nonprofit educational corporation whose goals are to develop an educational and crosscultural perspective linking various scientific, social, and artistic fields; to nurture a holistic view of arts, sciences, humanities, and healing; and to publish and distribute literature on the relationship of mind, body, and nature.

PLEASE NOTE: The creators and publishers of this book are not and will not be responsible, in any way whatsoever, for any improper use made by anyone of the information contained in this book. All use of the aforementioned information must be made in accordance with what is permitted by law, and any damage liable to be caused as a result thereof will be the exclusive responsibility of the user. In addition, he or she must adhere strictly to the safety rules contained in the book, both in training and in actual implementation of the information presented herein. This book is intended for use in conjunction with ongoing lessons and personal training with an authorized expert. It is not a substitute for formal training. It is the sole responsibility of every person planning to train in the techniques described in this book to consult a licensed physician in order to obtain complete medical information on his or her personal ability and limitations. The instructions and advice printed in this book are not in any way intended as a substitute for medical, mental, or emotional counseling with a licensed physician or healthcare provider.

This book is dedicated in memory of my late husband,
teacher, and best friend, Sifu Kuo Lien-Ying.

Dedication plaque for Kuo family
at Chinese for Affirmative Action Building of San Francisco

# ACKNOWLEDGMENTS

If not for the teachings, guidance and encouragement of a great Master of Tai-Chi Chuan, Sifu Kuo Lien-Ying, this book would be just pages in my mind. It was he who moved me to go on this journey. The material in this book was provided by him in hopes that this valuable information would be passed on to the new generation.

My son, Chung-Mei Kuo, belongs here as well. For it was watching his great performances of Tai-Chi Chuan at a very early age that gave me courage and inspiration.

Special thanks to these honorable students who sustained and supported our studio at the beginning in 1965:

| | |
|---|---|
| Harry Choy | Yow Lee |
| Chuck Lee | Milton Owyang |
| Hank Wong | Gene Wong |
| Chuck Thompson | David Chin |
| Sing-Poy Lee | Halford Kekuewa |

Thanks to Jeffrey Kessler and Pauline Luk for editing, and to Bill Hazelwood for photography. Thanks to my students, who were enthusiastic and willing to assist in every way they could.

| | |
|---|---|
| Barbara Riddle Cellers | Sheila Luttringer |
| Danny Kent | Jeffrey Chiang |
| Catherine Cunningham | Yi-sung Lei |
| Mary Jane Tiernan | Francis Monet Carter |
| Ron Suther | Jonathan Schwartz |

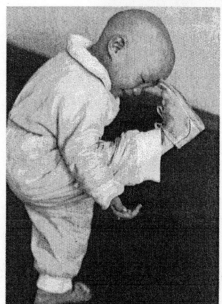

Chung-Mei Kuo was a great performer
at a young age.

# TABLE OF CONTENTS

# PREFACE
# TAI-CHI CHUAN

You have been given a gift! A gift of timeless elegance. A complete system of what on the surface looks like just exercise, but in reality is also philosophical, metaphysical, and psychophysiological.

What is Tai-Chi Chuan? (From all persons one can elicit different answers.) It is therapy, meditation, self-defense, energy, balance, and symbology. It is the "cosmic dance".

The daily practice of Tai-Chi Chuan will unite the intrinsic with the extrinsic: the Yin with the Yang. In its consummate beauty it adapts to each individual's temperament, body, and spirit. We are put in touch with the world without, as well as the world deep within. (It is the within/without, each giving appropriate acknowledgement to the other, that determines the quality of life.)

Through physical commitment we learn the meaning of the Yang and the Yin: the hard and the soft, the positive and the negative, Heaven and Earth. The ultimate significance of understanding the light and dark tends to form a certain clarity, not of antagonism, but rather of the balancing of the two universal energies.

In *Island* Aldous Huxley presents a possible mechanism of Utopia:

"What sort of dance does he teach?" Mrs. Naravan tried to describe it, "No leaps, no high kicks, no running. The feet always firmly on the ground . . . movements intrinsically beautiful and at the same time charged with symbolic meaning. Thought taking shape in ritual and stylized gesture. The whole body transformed into a hieroglyph, a succession of hieroglyphs, of attitudes modulating from significance to significance, like a poem or a piece of music. Movements of the muscles representing movements of the consciousness. . . . It's meditation in action." She concluded, "It's the metaphysics of the Mahayana expressed not in words, but through symbolic movements and gestures."

The practice of Tai-Chi Chuan requires not words, not music; nothing that is not already within. It is practiced in total silence requiring only one's own deep sense of commitment. There is nothing mystical here, and most importantly for the beginner, Tai-Chi Chuan is not an abstraction. It is intensely pragmatic and experimental.

You have given *yourself* the gift: personal benefit.

**Dr. Eric Paul Shaber**

# FOREWORD

It is almost impossible to write about Tai-Chi Chuan without sounding like a fanatic. Personal testimonials about Tai-Chi Chuan's miraculous effects abound. I could add my own particulars to the list — the disappearance of a chronic back problem, for example — but instead, I will describe the gradual process by which Tai-Chi Chuan has become part of my life with the hope of providing an introduction to the experience for someone interested in studying Tai-Chi Chuan.

I began to take lessons from the author of this book at the time that I began work on my Ph.D. dissertation. As a scholar in the Humanities, I sought to comprehend the "meaning" of Tai-Chi Chuan while I learned the series of exercises. I struggled against the necessity of following strict instructions which were not accompanied by reasoned explanations. During this period, Tai-Chi Chuan filled my need for physical exercise like any class in dance or gymnastics, but because it demanded daily practice, it also provided a strong dose of discipline. Since Tai-Chi Chuan is an explicitly ordered set of movements, I could accomplish something definite each day before embarking upon my seemingly endless academic work.

While relying on Tai-Chi Chuan to structure my daily routine, I began to accept the pace and rhythm of this ancient Chinese martial art. I stopped demanding that there be certain measurable signs of my achievement; I allowed the rewards to be revealed rather than expected. I found that this attitude permitted constant progress without competitive tests to prove my competence. Whereas I had been waiting for some miraculous spurt of new energy, I started then to acknowledge the value of the countless, imperceptibly small changes brought about by the repetition of the movements. I felt healthy; I gained strength and flexibility, and I developed a sense of bodily awareness. At this point, I no longer needed to be reminded to practice every day and knew that I was hooked.

Now, whether I exercise alone or with a class, Tai-Chi Chuan helps to rejuvenate my spirits, calm my nerves, and clear my mind while, at the same time, my body stretches and relaxes. The desire to understand Tai-Chi Chuan intellectually has been supplanted by a desire to do Tai-Chi Chuan actively, perhaps most simply because it is useful.

**Ellen Woods, Ph.D.**
Stanford University

# AN INTRODUCTION TO THE KUO FAMILY

Simmone Kuo is a master of Tai-Chi Chuan, Shao-Lin Chuan, the staff, the broad sword, and the Tai-Chi sword. Currently the instructor at the Tai-Chi Chuan Academy at 15-A Walter U. Lum Place in San Francisco, California, she has written and performed a series of television programs on Tai-Chi Chuan which has been broadcast nationally. She has also served on the faculty of the Physical Education Department at San Francisco State University since 1980, teaching Tai-Chi Chuan.

Mrs. Kuo's husband, the late Kuo Lien-Ying, was an international figure in the martial arts community. A practitioner of the arts for more than 70 years, a living legend of his time, Sifu Kuo was also a congressman in the National Assembly of China. He taught the traditional style of Tai-Chi Chuan that has been handed down unchanged over the ages.

Sifu and Simu Kuo have one son, Chung-Mei, born in 1967, who began practicing Tai-Chi Chuan as soon as he could walk.

Few teachers of Tai-Chi Chuan can match Simu Kuo's energy, simplicity, and clarity of style. Simu's constant efforts to improve and demystify this art have earned her a growing popularity. She has been very successful in interpreting Tai-Chi Chuan for Americans through television, publications, and numerous classes in colleges, universities, and other educational institutions.

In 1977, the Chinese Culture Foundation presented a series of multicultural training programs for secondary teachers, reaching thirty-six schools under a project of the Office of Education. When we approached Simu to teach Tai-Chi Chuan, she was enthused and generously shared with us her accumulated experience, knowledge, and materials. Upon completion of the training sessions, a *Teacher's Handbook on Tai-Chi Chuan* was produced which was so popular that it was quickly sold out. We are, therefore, greatly pleased that Simu is now publishing an expanded version of that book so that many more may benefit both spiritually and physically from this enduring and ancient Chinese physical art form.

**Dr. Shirley Sun**
Executive Director
Chinese Culture Foundation 1979

# I

# A BRIEF HISTORY OF CHINESE MARTIAL ARTS

The origin of the martial arts can be traced back to the very beginning of human culture in ancient China. According to legend, the creator of heaven and earth gave human beings the responsibility of ruling the earth. However, by the time human beings appeared, animals of every description were already well established and able to defend their territories by the methods which are special to each kind: force, speed, camouflage, and so on. Human beings also had a special talent; the talent of being able to learn from every aspect of their environment. The martial arts developed, then, from observation and imitation of nature: the stillness of mountains, the fluidity of rivers, the motion of the stars. In the difficult struggle for existence, human beings were also drawn to imitate the movements and actions of the very animals with which they had to contend: tigers, monkeys, birds, snakes, insects, and all the others. Such is the origin of the martial arts.

Every part of ancient China had its own native fighting forms. Early martial artists gradually grouped the movements they had learned from observation of nature into harmonious series or sets. As time continued, martial artists also adopted the use of such weapons as knives, swords, and spears.

## SOURCES OF TAI-CHI CHUAN

During the 5th century AD, the Buddhist monk Bodhidharma (Ta-mo)[1] journeyed from India to China, where he travelled extensively and taught for many years. In particular, he stayed for several years at the Shao-Lin Temple in Honan Province of central China, teaching the Buddhist sutras and meditation. Finding that the sedentary life often left the monks weak

---

[1]Bodhidharma, or as the Chinese call him, Ta-mo, was also the first patriarch of the Zen (Chan) school of Buddhism.

both in body and mind, Ta-mo decided to encourage physical discipline as well as meditation. He taught the stretching exercises from the Indian tradition of yoga with which he was familiar. On their part, the Chinese monks were reminded of the native fighting forms of their youth. A group of eighteen particularly dedicated monks then developed and refined a system of stretching exercises and movements which is the core of what is now known as Shao-Lin Chuan,[2] the source for all subsequent martial arts, including Tai-Chi Chuan. The Chinese revere the eighteen monks to this day and venerate them as Lohans.[3]

In 722 AD, the monks of Shao-Lin Temple received special acclaim when they performed admirably in response to an appeal by Emperor Tang Hsuan-Tsung, who was conducting a campaign in that area. Thereafter, Shao-Lin Temple became famous as the cradle of Chinese Chuan Shu, or martial arts.[4]

During the Yuan Dynasty (1279-1368 AD), Shao-Lin Chuan was further refined, and the series of basic movements was expanded. Today, there exist hundreds of different forms of Shao-Lin Chuan, which comprise what is called the "external" or "outer" school of Chuan Shu. These forms stress the development of strength, speed, and endurance. The "outer" school seeks primarily to develop the physical body, in contrast to "inner" spiritual cultivation. Therefore, the different forms of Shao-Lin Chuan all stress quick movements, leaps, and kicks. The "outer" school of Chuan Shu has also spread to neighboring Asian countries, stimulating the development of such forms as the Japanese karate and the Korean Tae Kwan Do.[5]

From Shao-Lin Chuan also developed an "internal" or "inner" school of Chuan Shu. In martial arts, the term "inner" has two meanings. One refers to the systems of exercise which strengthen the internal organs of the body and improve their functions. These systems stress the coordination of natural breathing with movement and are considered best for promoting good health. But "inner" also has a second, deeper meaning: it refers to the development of mind and spirit, and how these may become manifest through concentrated

---

[2]Shao-lin Chuan: Shao-lin = youth; chuan = fist, symbol of the martial arts. Hence, Shao-lin Chuan are martial arts for the young.

[3]Lohans are special heroes, people who have succeeded in channelling their selfish and destructive energies into work for the benefit of all.

[4]Chuan Shu: Chuan = fist; shu = arts. Chuan Shu is the general term for all the Chinese martial arts.

[5]The term Kung Fu is often used in the West to name the "outer" school of Chuan Shu. In Chinese, Kung Fu means skill acquired through time and practice; it can refer to any activity (e.g. calligraphy), not only the martial arts.

movement. In this type of practice, although one may appear still on the outside, he may be continuing to circulate his force within. In contrast to the outer school of Chuan Shu, forms of the "inner" school stress non-violent movement and the development of inner strength.

Pa-Kua Chang and Shing-Yi Chuan, two forms of the "inner" school, deserve mention here because, together with Shao-Lin Chuan, they provided the source movements for Tai-Chi Chuan, the most popular and most highly developed form of the "inner" school.

The basic exercise of Pa-Kua Chang[6] follows the curious, bobbing gait of the camel, which can walk in heavy sand and carry great weights for long periods of time without tiring. The circular movements of Pa-Kua Chang are very deft and light. Their fluid changes around the circle also embody the principles and philosophy of the eight basic trigrams of the *I Ching*, the famous Chinese *Book of Changes*.

Shing-Yi Chuan[7] takes its idea from the movements of various animal prototypes—creatures of the sea, the land, and the air. From each creature, Shing-Yi Chuan borrows the unique secret of its self-defense. From the snake, for example, the practitioner learns to move swiftly through the smallest opening. The movements of Shing-Yi Chuan are rather fast and quite varied, resembling in this respect the "outer" styles of Chuan Shu. But, as is true of all the "inner" styles, in Shing-Yi it is the mind which remains the prime mover.

# THE CREATION OF TAI-CHI CHUAN

Of the "inner" styles of Chuan Shu, Tai-Chi Chuan is deservedly the most famous. Because of its gentle nature, Tai-Chi Chuan is accessible to people of all ages and temperaments. It was the intention of the creators of Tai-Chi Chuan to fashion a set of flowing, natural movements from which all

---

[6]Pa-Kua Chang: Pa = 8; Kua = trigram; Chang = palm. Pa-Kua Chang is based on the arrangement of the 8 trigrams of the *I Ching* around the Tai-Chi circle (see diagram 2). It is referred to as "palm" rather than "fist" because Pa-Kua style stresses the use of the open hand.

[7]Shing-Yi Chuan: difficult to translate. Shing-Yi = movements which are based on ideas; Chuan = fist. Shing-Yi style seeks to discover the principles of nature and to express them in lines of movement.

might benefit, according to their abilities and their interests.

Most histories place the creation of Tai-Chi Chuan with Chang San-Feng of the Yuan and the beginning of the Ming Dynasty in the 14th century AD. Chang was originally from Long-Sun Mountain in Shensi province. As a young man, Chang practiced and mastered the "outer" styles of Chuan Shu. Later he became a well-known body guard of the nobility in Beijing. After leaving his post in the Emperor's court, Chang retired to the countryside of his youth, living as a recluse in the mountains. There, together with a group of old masters, which included Lee Tao-Tse, he dedicated himself to the creation of a non-violent form of practice from which people of all ages could benefit. In order to do so, they drew from Shao-Lin Chuan, Shing-Yi Chuan, and Pa-Kua Chang, synthesizing the essentials of each style through personal research and experiment, into what we today know as Tai-Chi Chuan.

This account of Tai-Chi Chuan's beginnings comes to us principally from Wang Tsung-Yue, an early practitioner of the art, who was also a skilled writer. He compiled the *Tai-Chi Chuan Dictionary*, which deals with the principles of the art and has proved very useful to succeeding generations in understanding the fundamental methods and their application. Fortunately, the book has been handed down and is still available today.

Tai-Chi Chuan became increasingly popular, and towards the end of the Ming Dynasty (17th century AD), the emperor strongly encouraged scholars and others to begin practicing the art. He sent Chen Wang-Ting, a person well-versed in both literary and martial arts, to tour the countryside of China and research the existing forms of Tai-Chi Chuan. Chen found that Chia-Go of Honan province had the most complete and accurate movements. He based this conclusion on the *Book of Fist* by Ch'i Chi-Kuang (1528–1587) a famous general of the Ming period. Known in Chinese as the *Chuan Ching (Classic of Pugilism)*, Ch'i's book contains exhaustive records and descriptions of all the forms of Chuan Shu then current in China.

In the 19th century (Ch'ing Dynasty), Yang Ban-Ho, a student of the Chen family in Honan, came to Beijing where he opened a school. From Yang and his famous student Wang Chiao-Yu comes the traditional form of Tai-Chi Chuan which we know today. Wang was Yang's best student, diligent and devoted in his practice, careful to preserve Yang's teaching without any changes. Wang attained great success, and his reputation went far and wide.

In his old age, Wang lived at the Lu-Tsu Temple in the Ho-ping-men (Door of Peace) sector of Beijing. There he had a studio where he dedicated his time and efforts to teaching. It was to this great master that the young Kuo Lien-Ying came to study Tai-Chi Chuan in the early part of the 20th century. Kuo found that, though Wang was quite advanced in years (ninety-four), his spirit was tremendously strong and bright. He walked with a stride "as if he were flying," according to Kuo.

A congressman to the National Assembly of China, Kuo left his homeland in 1952, travelling to Taiwan, where he settled and taught Tai-Chi Chuan until 1965. Before leaving Taiwan, Kuo married Simmone Lu. Together they came to the United States and in 1966 established the Lien-Ying Tai-Chi Chuan Academy in San Francisco's Chinatown. In 1983 Kuo Lien-Ying returned to China where he died in 1984. He was honored with a state funeral.

Under the tutelage of her husband, Mrs. Kuo studied both traditional Chinese philosophy and Tai-Chi Chuan, as well as numerous other forms of Chuan Shu, from both the "outer" and the "inner" schools. The current book represents the distillation of that experience, together with the results of Mrs. Kuo's extensive research into the best methods for teaching Tai-Chi Chuan here in the West. Mrs. Kuo continues to teach at the Academy and at San Francisco State University, where she has been on the faculty since 1980.

* * *

In present-day China, Tai-Chi Chuan is the most widely practiced of the traditional martial arts. It has been revived and incorporated into general physical education programs throughout the land. Tai-Chi Chuan's greatness lies in its combining both mental and spiritual forces within a simple physical practice. Its gentle and supple movements are unequalled for promoting good health and total well-being.

# YIN-YANG
# AND TAI-CHI PHILOSOPHY

The philosophers of ancient China believed that, in the beginning, the world was void and boundless. This state they called "wu chi." Out of the void, they hypothesized, arose two primal forces: yang and yin, positive and negative. The union of yin and yang forms what the Chinese call Tai-Chi, which was later represented visually by what is known to the West as the Yin/Yang symbol. (See Yin & Yang Diagram 1.)

The word "Tai-Chi" is made up of two Chinese characters, "Tai" (太), which means vast and all-encompassing, and "Chi" (極), which means the ultimate or extreme point. In Chinese philosophy, "Tai-Chi" refers to the absolute or ultimate point of the universe, which is thought to be forever constant and to exist in all things. Analogous to the Western symbol of the cross, which can be understood as the intersection of the horizontal (tai) and vertical (chi) dimensions of existence, Tai-Chi refers to the manifestation of the absolute, present at the heart of each and every phenomenon. Nothing in the manifest universe, then, is pure yin or pure yang. Each created being embodies a dynamic balance of yin and yang energies. Unlike the cross, which expresses a kind of static tension at the center of all existence, the Tai-Chi symbol emphasizes the dynamic and changing quality of the universe. The symbol is divided into two sectors of force which do not oppose but complement each other to form a bi-une whole.

Reflecting deeply on the natural world, the philosophers of ancient China perceived the interconnectedness of all things. They understood that the changes in this shifting whole could be viewed as the two primal forces, yin and yang, complementing and transmuting into one another, so that their interplay permeates all of creation. Each of the Tai-Chi symbol's complementary teardrops—one light, yang; the other dark, yin—includes at its center a point of the complementary force. Thus, each of the two forces is transformed in nature when it is fully achieved. After a sufficient period of rest (yin), for example, activity (yang) spontaneously arises. And activity (yang) cannot go on indefinitely, but must give way to stillness (yin).

6

YIN & YANG DIAGRAM 1

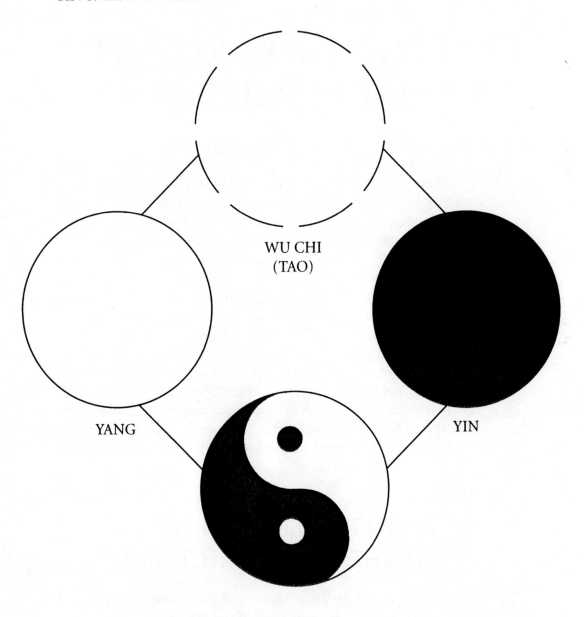

WU CHI
(TAO)

YANG

YIN

TAI-CHI

# TAI-CHI CHUAN RELATED TO TAI-CHI PHILOSOPHY

Whereas the term "Tai-Chi" refers to the ancient philosophical idea, the term "Tai-Chi Chuan" refers to the martial art (chuan) which is based on this philosophy. In Tai-Chi Chuan, the objective is not to over-exert or to strain one's natural state, but to achieve unity with one's essential nature, thereby releasing the body's intrinsic energy.

The complementarity and transmutability of the two primal forces are exhibited in the Tai-Chi Chuan movements, which are circular and shift with fluidity and grace from one to the next. Feet, knees, legs, waist, hands, and head move in harmonious sequence, changing from yin to yang and yang to yin. Yang is yin in motion, yin is yang at rest. Hard is yang, soft is yin. Fast is yang, slow is yin. In practicing Tai-Chi Chuan, the goal is to achieve a dynamic balance of the two primal forces, and so to embody the Tai-Chi which is their fusion. Therefore, the traditional style is not too fast, not too slow in pace; not too hard, not too soft in manner of execution. And just as, according to Tai-Chi philosophy, "all things are continuously moving and restless, yet each is proceeding back to the source," so the sequence of movements we call Tai-Chi Chuan ends as it began, standing still in a posture both relaxed and alert.

# FIVE ELEMENT THEORY AND THE EIGHT TRIGRAMS

Five Element Theory and the Eight Trigrams of the *I Ching* are two related symbolic systems which developed out of the core of Tai-Chi philosophy. According to the ancient philosophers, after fusing to form the Tai-Chi, the two primal forces, yin and yang, generate by their interaction the five directions of the universe, each of which creates one of the five basic elements of nature:

the center, which creates earth

| | |
|---|---|
| east | wood |
| west | gold |
| south | fire |
| north | water |

Tai-Chi Chuan uses this aspect of Five Element Theory to describe the directions of possible movement:[1]

| | |
|---|---|
| gold | advance |
| wood | retreat |
| water | shift to left |
| fire | shift to right |
| earth | on guard, in the center |

The Eight Trigrams of the *I Ching* are also understood to be generated by the transmutations of yin and yang energy. Diagram 2 shows how the trigrams may be arranged around the Tai-Chi circle, illustrating the movement from yin to yang and yang to yin. By combining any two of these trigrams to form a six-line figure, 64 possible combinations are obtained. These are the 64 hexagrams of the *I Ching*, said to represent all possible states of change in the universe. Therefore, the traditional form of Tai-Chi Chuan consists of exactly 64 movements.

DIAGRAM 2

---

[1]Five Element Theory also forms the basis for the Chinese medical system of diagnosis and treatment. Each of the five elements is associated with one of the major organ systems of the body. Those interested can find further information in the *Yellow Emperor's Book*, or in any manual of traditional acupuncture.

# THE BENEFITS
# OF TAI-CHI CHUAN

Tai-Chi Chuan differs from other forms of exercise in its holistic approach. Every movement of Tai-Chi Chuan involves the entire body. The primary aim of Tai-Chi Chuan is to allow the person through physical activity to develop the natural rhythm and sense of his body, and to harmonize the actions of the body with those of the mind.

Tai-Chi Chuan is excellent for strengthening the body on many different levels. Its movements are slow-paced and not strenuous. The practice of Tai-Chi Chuan does not tax the body; rather it creates strength and energy. The movements give every part of the body — muscles, bones, and joints — a chance to exercise; and they also improve the natural functions of the organs, increasing their vigor and strengthening them against disease.

In addition to controlled motions and natural breathing, Tai-Chi Chuan also requires tranquility and concentration of the mind. In the practice of Tai-Chi Chuan, all spirit and thought must be concentrated within oneself. This is good discipline for the mind. In addition, since all movements have to be done in an integrated fashion, the practice of Tai-Chi Chuan leads to improved awareness of the different parts of the body, and better functioning of the central nervous system.

Tai-Chi Chuan will foster such positive qualities as calmness, perseverance, patience, and determination. If practiced conscientiously, Tai-Chi Chuan will lead to both mental and physical well-being, improved health, and may even lengthen one's life significantly.

Master Kuo Lien-Ying back in his hometown
Hu Ho Hao Te, Inner Mongolia, 1976.

# II

# PREPARATORY NOTES BEFORE PRACTICE

Tai-Chi Chuan is a form of exercise designed for men and women of all ages. For those young and healthy, there are no problems in starting the practice of Tai-Chi Chuan at any time. It is advisable that older people with chronic conditions (such as high blood pressure or heart disease) have a checkup with their doctor before consulting a Tai-Chi Chuan instructor. Instructors with sufficient years of training[1] in Tai-Chi Chuan are sensitive to the individual health needs of their students and give special consideration to their welfare.

When practicing Tai-Chi Chuan, one should wear clothing which permits easy movement. It is best to exercise wearing a sweatshirt and sweatpants or other loose-fitting garments. In the choice of shoes, attention should be paid to a good fit and lightness of weight. Tennis shoes are appropriate. One should not practice in shoes with heels or those with a hard sole. In the wintertime, it is all right to wear hat and gloves for protection against the cold. Long underwear is also appropriate in such weather. These items do not hamper the movement of the body. After exercising, it is quite natural for the body to perspire. Students should be careful not to take off their warm clothes immediately, as this could lead to colds and chills. A brief walk (in silence) after practicing helps the body to regulate its temperature naturally.

Tai-Chi Chuan instructors will advise their students as to the length of the practice, and will teach new movements according to the individual student's age, physical condition, ability, and stage of emotional development. It is important that both students and instructors keep this in mind.

Tai-Chi Chuan can be practiced indoors, but the most ideal location would be out of doors, in a park or in the open air. Tai-Chi Chuan can be

---

[1]One indicator of the time a person has devoted to the practice of Tai-Chi Chuan is that person's spinal flexibility; this is normally demonstrated in the "chin to toe" exercise (to be described later in the text).

practiced at any hour of the day; however, the best time is the very early morning between 5 and 8 o'clock. The air is usually freshest at this time, especially in congested urban areas.

It is well to maintain silence shortly before and after, as well as during the practice of Tai-Chi Chuan. The mind remains quiet and alert, with attention focused on the movements and the positions. The movements should be done as an integrated whole, and not as isolated or disjointed steps. No movement should be forced or strained.

# MAJOR DIFFICULTIES

1. In Tai-Chi Chuan every single movement must involve the entire body. Tai-Chi Chuan beginners often forget to move the right and left hands simultaneously, or to move the hands and the legs simultaneously.

2. In usual standing positions, the weight of the body is carried by both legs. When practicing Tai-Chi Chuan, the person must be able to distinguish between "hollow" and "solid." In other words, one leg will be bent in order to support the weight of the whole body, while the other leg is in a "hollow" state. Generally, people are not accustomed to such positions when they first practice Tai-Chi Chuan.

3. When practicing Tai-Chi Chuan, the practitioner must breathe naturally in addition to matching the movements evenly with the breathing. This is difficult for most beginners. It should be mentioned that beginning difficulties are common in Tai-Chi Chuan, and after the student practices regularly, these difficulties will diminish.

To increase confidence on the part of beginning students, excessive demands should not be made on their performance of movements and breathing. Beginners will slowly develop confidence by careful practice and repetition of the Tai-Chi Chuan movements. Success will not come quickly, nor will it come if one quits half-way. Students must know that the beginning period is quite difficult, but that after they are exposed to Tai-Chi Chuan and are able to grasp its principles, they can achieve its light and nimble body movements.

As far as teachers are concerned, there should be a teaching method and lesson plans according to individual needs. When giving lectures, do not over-emphasize or over-exaggerate difficulties which might frighten students. Every gesture and movement should be taught separately according to the student's progress.

# SCHEDULE FOR LEARNING TAI-CHI CHUAN

The learning of Tai-Chi Chuan is a lifelong process that one cultivates through consistent and persevering practice. In a period of about nine or ten months, one can learn the ten basic exercises and the sixty-four movements of the Tai-Chi Chuan set. The sixty-four movements are divided into four quarters. To establish the best learning pace, we propose a schedule as follows:

1st Quarter:
Warm-Up Exercises 1– 6
 (1) Rotating Waist
 (2) Rotating Hips
 (3) Rotating Knees
 (4) Palm to Floor
 (5) Side Leg Stretch
 (6) Chin to Toe
Movements 1–14

2nd Quarter:
Warm-Up Exercises 7–10
 (7) Diagonal kick
 (8) Straight-ahead kick (heel up, toe down)
 (9) Hand-slapping kick with toe pointing forward
 (10) Double kick with two feet off ground
Movements 15–32

3rd Quarter:
Movements 33–46

4th Quarter:
Movements 47–64

After completing each quarter there should be a one-week break.

# A COMPLETE LIST OF THE SIXTY-FOUR TAI-CHI CHUAN MOVEMENTS AS HANDED DOWN BY KUO LIEN-YING

## 太極拳正宗六十四式 郭連蔭傳

1. Strike palm to ask Buddha
2. Grasp bird's tail
3. Single whip
4. Stork spreads wings
5. Brush knee and twist step
6. Deflect downward, parry and punch
7. Step up and push with palm
8. Carry tiger to mountain
9. Fist under elbow
10. Step back and repulse monkey
11. Slow palm slanting, flying
12. Raise right (left) hand
13. Fly pulling back and step up
14. Fan through the arm
15. Green dragon dropping water
16. Single whip
17. Wave hands like clouds
18. Single whip
19. High pat on horse
20. Separation of right (left) foot
21. Turn and kick with sole
22. Wind blowing lotus leaf
23. Finger block up with fist
24. Turn around and kick two feet upward
25. Step up, deflect downward, parry and punch
26. Step back with arms beside body
27. Left foot kicks up, forward
28. Turn and kick with sole
29. Step forward, deflect downward, parry and punch
30. Pull back with palm and push
31. Carry tiger to mountain
32. Chop opponent with fist
33. Diagonal single whip
34. Partition of wild horse's mane
35. Diagonal single whip
36. Working at shuttles inside clouds
37. Step up and grasp bird's tail
38. Single whip
39. Wave hands like clouds
40. Single whip lowering down
41. Golden cock stands on one leg
42. Step back and repulse monkey
43. Slow palm slanting, flying
44. Raise right (left) hand
45. Fly pulling back and step up
46. Fan through arms
47. Strike opponent's ears with both fists
48. Through sky cannon
49. Single whip
50. Wave hands like clouds
51. Single whip
52. High pat on horse
53. Cross wave of water lily
54. Downward fist
55. Step up and grasp bird's tail
56. Single whip
57. Wave hands like clouds
58. Single whip lowering down
59. Step up to form seven stars
60. Retreat to right tiger
61. Slanting body and turn the moon
62. Wave lotus foot
63. Shoot tiger with bow and arrow
64. Right (left) grasp bird's tail

Conclusion of grand terminus

# 太極六十四式

太極正宗　郭連蔭

一、擊掌問佛
二、攬雀尾
三、單鞭
四、白鶴掠翅
五、摟膝拗步
六、却步搬攔捶
七、上步如封似閉
八、抱虎歸山
九、肘底錘
十、倒攆猴
十一、左右斜飛
十二、挫掌提手
十三、飛攆臂
十四、扇通臂
十五、青龍出水
十六、單鞭
十七、雲手
十八、單鞭
十九、高探馬
二十、左右分脚
二一、轉身蹬脚
廿二、風擺荷葉
廿三、指擋捶
廿四、翻身二起脚
廿五、上步搬攔捶
廿六、退步搬攔捶
廿七、迎面踢脚
廿八、轉身蹬脚
廿九、進步搬攔捶
三十、如封似閉
三一、抱虎歸山
三二、撤身捶
三三、斜單鞭
三四、野馬分鬃
三五、斜單鞭
三六、雲裡穿梭
三七、轉身攬雀尾
三八、單鞭
三九、雲手
四十、單鞭下勢
四一、金鷄獨立
四二、倒攆猴
四三、挫掌斜飛
四四、左右提手
四五、飛攆臂
四六、扇通臂
四七、雙風貫耳
四八、通天炮
四九、單鞭
五十、雲手
五一、高探馬
五二、十字擺蓮
五三、栽捶
五四、十字擺蓮
五五、上步攬雀尾
五六、單鞭
五七、雲手
五八、單鞭下勢
五九、上步七星
六十、退步跨虎
六一、斜身扭跨月
六二、擺蓮脚
六三、彎弓射虎
六四、左右攬雀尾
　　合太極

# BEGIN 1ST QUARTER

## Exercises 1–6

## Movements 1–14

# PREPARATORY EXERCISES
## (Warm-Up Exercises 1–6)

## 1. Waist and Stomach Rotating Exercise 柔腰

Stand straight, with feet together, hands on waist, and fingers facing each other at the small of the back. The thumbs are forward, the four fingers on the back. (See Pictures 1A-front and 1A-back) Use fingers to push the stomach forward, and start rotating in circular movements: 32 times to the right, and 32 times to the left.

Note: Keep the knees straight but not locked. This exercise aids digestion and strengthens the waist and stomach muscles.

1A-front          1A-back

## 2. Hip Rotating Exercise 柔跨

Stand straight, with feet parallel and one foot apart. (This can be marked off by first putting the heel of the right foot in the arch of the left foot and rotating the right foot into a parallel stance.) (See Picture 2A) Put the hands on the lower hip, with fingers towards the back and pointing down. The thumbs are forward, the four fingers on the back. Use the left hand to push the hip towards the right, and rotate hips in an oval movement: 32 times to right, 32 times to left. This exercise helps in loosening the hip joints.

2A          2B

# 3. Knee Rotating Exercise 柔膝

Stand straight, with feet together and knees bent. Put the hands on the knees, with fingers open and elbows straight. Keep the back straight and the chin up. (See Pictures 3A-front and 3A-side) In the beginning, rotate the knees in a circular motion six times to the right, and then six times to the left. This exercise is hard to do, but try to work up to 20 rotations in each direction by the end of one month, and up to 32 by the end of two months. When finished, use the palms to push the knees straight back, keeping the back straight and the chin up, and stay in this position for one minute. (See Picture 3B)

It is important to keep the knees bent and the elbows straight while exercising. This exercise strengthens the ankle and knee joints and aids in balance.

3A-front              3A-side              3B

# 4. Palm to the Ground Exercise 手心貼地

Stand straight, feet together, chin up, and arms extended overhead. Clasp fingers with palms facing the sky. (See Picture 4A) Lean from the waist, from side to side, keeping the elbows straight. Do this three times to stretch the sides of the chest and arms. (See Picture 4B) Then, still keeping the elbows and knees straight, bend forward as far as possible. After some practice, it will be easy to touch the ground with the palms or even with the elbows; but in the beginning, do not force the palms down. Instead, bounce gently up and down to stretch the back muscles. (See Picture 4C)

It is important not to force the palms to the floor. It is more important to do this exercise correctly; touching the ground will come naturally. (See Picture 4D) Remember to keep the knees straight and the head up. This exercise stretches the muscles of the sides and the back.

4A                    4B

4C                    4D

## 5. Side Leg Stretch Exercise
# 仆腿

Spread legs with knees bent, feet parallel approximately two shoulder widths apart, and hands on the knees. The knees are noticeably bent, and the body is slightly forward. (See Picture 5A) Then, bend the right knee as far as possible while rotating the body to the left, keeping the feet parallel. (See Picture 5B) This exercise stretches the legs. Do the same for the right leg, bending the left knee and rotating the body to the right. (See Picture 5C)

It is important to remember that this is a very difficult exercise to do properly. Do not force the stretching. In the beginning it is permissible to hold on for support. (See Picture 5D)

5A

5B

5C

5D

# 6. Chin to the Toe Exercise 金鷄啄食

This exercise used to be called "Golden Cock Pecking at Food." Stand straight, with feet together and the left foot turned 45 degrees outward. Step forward with the right foot approximately two feet in front, with heel down and toes up. All the weight is on the back foot. Bend forward from the waist, keeping the right leg straight and the left leg bent, and put both hands on the right knee. (See Picture 6A) If you can, reach down with both hands and pull back the right foot. As you stretch, keep the chin up. Then, do the same for the left leg. Step forward with the left foot, bend forward and put both hands on the left knee. In the beginning, simply bounce the body up and down several times, stretching the leg tendons. After a year or more of practice, it will be possible to touch the chin to the toe. (See Picture 6B) However, do not force the body into this position unnaturally.

beginning position for exercise 6

6A                    6-side                    6B

Note: It is very important to practice these exercises every day. They will both make the body feel good and limber up the muscles, tendons, and joints. It is more important to do the exercises continually and properly than to strain in any one of them.

# MOVEMENTS 1–14

## 1. Strike Palm to Ask Buddha 擊掌問佛

Stand straight, with hands at side and feet together. (See Picture 1A) Turn the right foot 45 degrees, bend both knees and extend the left foot forward approximately two feet, with the left knee straight, heel on the ground and toes up. (See Picture 1B) Raise both arms straight out at shoulder level. Turn palms to face front. (See Picture 1C) Bring the hands together in a circular motion at shoulder level, ending with the hands almost meeting one and one-half feet in front of the chest.[2] Keeping the hands open, bend the right hand at the wrist so that it is perpendicular to the middle of the left hand. (See Picture 1D) Hold this position.[3]

Note: Be sure that the hands and elbows are at shoulder level. Also make sure that the final positions of the arms form a circle.

1A

1B

[2]All such measurements must be adapted to the individual's body size and capabilities.

[3]From the beginning to the end of the Tai-Chi Chuan set, it is important to keep the fingers straight and the palms flat (unless the hand is fisted).

1C

1D

# 2. Grasp Bird's Tail 攬雀尾

From position 1, move left foot back past the right heel until it is 45 degrees in back of right foot. The left foot should be perpendicular to the right, and the right toes should point up. Slide both hands down to waist diagonally in front of the left hip, keeping both elbows slightly bent. The palm of the left hand faces up, while the palm of the right hand faces down. Keep the right leg straight and toes up. (See Picture 2A)

Then bring the right leg back so that the ball of the right foot touches the arch of the left foot. (See Picture 2B) Step forward with the right foot diagonally and bend both knees with weight centered and back straight. (See Picture 2C) From both elbows, raise hands to shoulder-height, and use the palms of both hands to push to the right side. (See Picture 2D) Both hands are parallel facing the diagonal, with elbows straight and right hand at the same angle as right foot. Twist the body at the waist and shoulders to make the hands even.

2A

2B

2C

2D

# 3. Single Whip 單 鞭

3A

From position 2, first turn the right toe inward. Now bring the left foot over to the right until the ball of the left foot touches near the arch of the right foot. Keep both knees bent, and move the right arm straight to the side and bend the hand down at the wrist. At the same time, bring the left arm to the chest, with the palm facing the left and touching the right shoulder. (See Picture 3A)

Then turn the head to the left, and step out with the left foot to the left side, bending both knees and keeping the weight centered. (See Picture 3B) Make sure that the feet are perpendicular to each other. Move the left hand out in a circular motion to the left, until the elbow is straight, then turn the palm so it faces left. (See Picture 3C)

3B

3C

# 4. Stork Spreads Wings 白鶴掠翅

From position 3, turn the left foot out (to the left). Bring the left hand down to the left hip with the elbow bent and palm facing downward. Step forward with the ball of the right foot, and swing the right hand around until it is in front of the body, with the elbow bent. The side of the right hand is chopping forward. The right heel is up. (See Picture 4A)

Bring the right foot back towards the left foot, then step out to the right side, while bringing the right elbow up to shoulder level, with the palm facing down. Step forward with the left foot in front of the body, with the heel up. (See Picture 4B)

4A          4A-front

4B          4B-front

# 5. Brush Knee and Twist Step 摟膝拗步

From position 4B, step back with left foot. (See Picture 5A) Turn right foot straight to body, bend knees, keeping the weight in the middle with hips and shoulders straight. Move both hands to right side with palms facing right, right elbow bent 90 degrees, and left arm bent at the wrist. (See Picture 5B)

Step back with right foot and turn left foot straight to body, bend knees and keep the weight in the middle. (See Picture 5C) Push to the left with both hands, now bending the left arm 90 degrees at elbow, right arm bent at wrist, and both palms facing left. (See Picture 5D)

5B      5A      4C

Note: Make sure that elbows and hands are kept level with the shoulders, and that the bent elbow and back form a straight line. Keep both hands away from the body and try not to tense the shoulders. Eventually, this movement should be done as a fluid whole with arms and legs moving simultaneously.

Also, when you step back with the left foot, make sure that it stays on the left side of the body's centerline. Similarly, when you step back with the right foot, it must remain on its own side.

5D      5C

# 6. Deflect Downward, Parry and Punch 却步搬攔捶

From position 5, make right hand into a fist and pull the arm down next to the right side of the body. Swing the left arm down until the open left hand is over the right wrist. Lastly, straighten the left knee and bring up the toes of left foot so that all the weight is on the right foot. (See Picture 6A)

Then punch forward in front of the body with both hands together while keeping weight centered and knees bent. (See Picture 6B) Note: Do not lean forward while punching. The body should be centered, the hips straight.

6A            6B

# 7. Step Up and Push with Palms 上步如封似閉

From position 6, open the right hand and pull both hands towards chest. At the same time, shift weight back on right leg until left knee straightens and left toes are up. Elbows should be slightly away from body, both hands under chin, palms facing out and making a triangle. (See Picture 7A) Both wrists are straight, and palms are flat.

Turn the left toes out, and step forward with right foot, making an L with the knees bent. Keep the hips and shoulders straight. (See Picture 7B) Now push forward with both hands at shoulder height until the elbows are straight and your hands no longer form a triangle. (See Picture 7C)

Note: When pushing, do not lean forward. The body should always be centered.

7A

7A-front

7B

7C

# 8. Carry Tiger to Mountain 抱虎歸山

From position 7, turn right toe in while forming a fist with the right hand. Turn the body around 180 degrees, simultaneously bringing the arms closer to the body. Keep the weight back, left toes up, left knee straight, and left hand open under right fist. (See Picture 8A) Open fist and move both hands forward, keeping elbows and wrists slightly bent. The third finger of the right hand lightly touches the palm of the left hand. (See Picture 8B) Note: Advanced students do not actually have hands touching, but keep them a half-inch apart.

Walk slowly starting with the left foot, while rotating hands in small clockwise circles. Walk as far as the space permits.[4] The clockwise movement is from the shoulders. When the left foot is forward, the hands are going down; when the right foot is forward, the hands are going up. (See Pictures 8C and 8D)

8A            8B

8C            8D

---

[4]All of the repeated movements (8, 10, 17, 22, 34, 41) can be performed as many times as space permits. the student must be careful, though, to end on the correct side.)

## 8. Carry Tiger to Mountain (continued) 抱虎歸山

Finish with the left foot forward, feet making an L, and punch with the right fist. Keep arms chest-high, right hand in a fist, and left hand open facing the body. The left elbow is slightly bent. (See Picture 8E)

8E

## 9. Fist Under Elbow 肘底錘

From the position shown in Picture 8E, open the right fist and bring the right hand towards the body, and then slap forward with the back of the right hand. Both the right elbow and wrist are straight. At the same time, turn the palm of the left hand up and bring the hand to the left side of the body slightly below the hip, keeping left elbow slightly bent. (See Picture 9)

9

# 10. Step Back and Repulse Monkey 倒攆猴

First Part: From position 9, turn the palm of the right hand down. At the same time, bring the left hand up to the left side of the chest, then turn the palm to the front. (See Picture 10A) Push straight forward with the left hand and shift the weight to the back. At the same time, bring the right hand down to the right side of the hip, with the palm facing down. The left knee is straight, the left toes up, and the right knee bent; weight is on the right leg. The shoulders and hips are straight. (See Picture 10B)

10A

10B-side view

10B

## 10. Step Back and Repulse Monkey (continued) 倒攆猴

Second Part: Turn both palms up at the same time. Raise right hand to chest and turn right palm facing front. (See Picture 10C) Step back with left foot and bring left hand to left side of hip while pushing forward with the right hand. Right knee and right arm are straight and right toes are up. Weight is on the left leg. (See Picture 10D)

Third Part: (This is a mirror image of the second part.) Turn right palm up; at the same time raise the left hand up to the chest and turn the palm facing front. (See Picture 10E) Step back with the right foot and bring the right hand to the right side of hip while pushing forward with the left hand. Left knee and arm are straight and left toes are up. (See Picture 10F) Alternate second and third parts three times each, ending with right arm extended. Note: The right palm faces down only in beginning position of first part.

10C

10D

10E

10F

# 11. Slow Palm Slanting Flying 挫掌斜飛

11A

From position shown in Picture 10D, bring the right foot back until the ball of the foot is next to the arch of the left foot, with the heel up. At the same time, put wrists together making an X, with right hand below facing up, and left hand above facing down. Keep both elbows slightly bent. (See Picture 11A)

Step forward diagonally 45 degrees with the right foot, and at the same time turn right palm so that it faces the body. The left foot will automatically turn out so that the two feet are perpendicular.

Spread out the hands, and bring them up to the shoulders like a bird spreading its wings. Keep the elbows straight and the right hand slightly higher than the left hand.

11B

Shoulders are down, hips and shoulders are straight to the body, and head is facing right. Palms face back. (See Picture 11C) Note: Make sure both knees are bent and weight is in the middle. Right hand should be in line with the right foot, and left hand in line with the middle of the left foot.

11C

# 12. Raise Right (Left) Hand 左右提手

Raise Right Hand: From the position shown in Picture 11B, keep the right foot stationary and step forward with the left foot, keeping the toes up and knee straight. Bring both hands to the front, right hand closer to the body and facing the left elbow. Keep both elbows bent. (See Picture 12A) Take a small step forward with the left foot, and at the same time, bring the ball of the right foot next to the arch of the left foot, keeping heel up. All the weight is on the left foot. Bring both hands together, brushing the palm of the left hand with the back of the right hand. (See Picture 12B) Continue raising the right hand until it is straight at shoulder level with palm facing down, and bring left hand to slightly below the waist with palm up. (See Picture 12C) Step back with right foot, and bring the hands back to the original position. (See Picture 12A)

12A

12B

12C

12A

# 12. Raise Right (Left) Hand (continued) 左右提手

Raise Left Hand: Now turn the body to the right 180 degrees, bringing the right toes up and right arm out farther than the left. The body is now a mirror image of Picture 12A. (See Picture 12D)

In the reverse of the first part, raise the left hand straight up to shoulder height, brushing past the right palm, and bring the right hand to the waist. (See Pictures 12E and 12F)

Step back, and at the same time bring the left hand past the right hand back to the beginning position of Picture 12D. The right toes are up and the right knee is straight.

Note: Make sure that the shoulders are straight.

12D          12D-front

12E          12F

## 13. Fly Pulling Back and Step Up

# 飛欄上勢

13A

From the position shown in Picture 12D, step forward slightly with right foot, while extending both arms forward until the elbows are straight, right palm down and left palm up. (See Picture 13A) Step back with right foot, bringing the ball of the right foot to the arch of the left foot. At the same time, bring both hands back with right forearm across the waist, and right palm facing the body. The left palm is at the left hip facing the right hand. (See Picture 13B)

Step forward with right foot, then bring up left foot until the ball of the foot is at the arch of the right foot. Raise the right arm to the chest, palm down, while keeping the left hand at the side. (See Picture 13C)

13B

13C

# 14. Fan Through the Arm 扇 通 臂

14A

From the position shown in Picture 13C, turn face to the left, then step to the left side with the left foot. Bend both knees and keep the weight in the center. The left toe is pointing left, forming a T to the right foot. (See Picture 14A) Moving both hands at the same time, bring the left arm up until it is straight from the shoulder with palm facing front, and bring the right hand back to the right side of the shoulder, the palm facing front. (See Pictures 14B front and back)

14B

14B-front

# End of 1st Quarter

# 踢腿

| | | |
|---|---|---|
| REVIEW<br>and<br>PRACTICE | 1– 6 Exercises<br>1–14 Movements | One Week |
| LEARN | 7–10 Exercises | |

Take care learning #10 — do not try to jump too high in the beginning. (The author is not responsible if the student falls and gets hurt.)

beginning exercise 6

# BEGIN 2ND QUARTER

## Exercises 7–10

## Movements 15–32

# WARM-UP EXERCISES 7–10

## 7. Diagonal Kicks 左右十字腿

Stand straight with both hands on the small of the back, thumbs forward, four fingers back, and feet together. Step forward 45 degrees to the left side with the left foot. (See Picture 7A) As soon as the left foot steps forward, continue in one motion to kick in the same diagonal direction with the right foot, keeping the knee straight and foot up. (See Picture 7B) End by bringing the right foot back to the left foot arch. Now do the reverse step 45 degrees to the right side with the right foot. (See Picture 7C) Kick with the left foot diagonally to the right side, bringing it back to the right foot arch. (See Picture 7D) Repeat 6 to 12 times.

Note: It is important to keep the hands on the small of the back, to keep the back straight, and to look in front while kicking. In the beginning, do not kick too high.

7A                    7B

7C                    7D

# 8. Straight Kick 踢勾腿
## (Toe Flexed and Toe Pointed)

Stand straight with both hands at center of back and feet together. Take a small step with the right foot (See Picture 8A) and kick straight up with the left foot, keeping the knee straight and the toes pointed up. (See Picture 8B) During the downward portion of the kick, flex the ankle to extend the toes of the foot forward. (See Picture 8C) End with the left toes touching the ground slightly in front of the body (See Picture 8D), then take a small step with the same foot, and kick with the right foot. Repeat kicks 6 to 12 times.

Note: Do not force the kicks, especially in the beginning. It is not important to kick very high.

8A          8B

8C          8D

# 9. Hand Slapping Foot Kick 踢拍平腿

Stand straight with the feet together and hands on either side, making fists at chest level. Take a small step with the right foot (See Picture 9A) and kick forward with the left foot. At the same time, open and extend the left hand, letting the hand and foot meet in front and making a slapping sound. (See Picture 9B) Bring the left hand back to its original position and end the kick with the left toe touching the floor slightly in front. (See Picture 9C) Now take a small step with the left foot, and repeat for the right side, kicking with the right leg and slapping the right foot with the right hand. (See Picture 9D) Continue for 6 to 12 kicks.

**Important:** Keep the knees straight and the feet extended when kicking. Do not force the slapping motions.

9A          9B

9C          9D

# 10. Double Kick 二起脚

Bring the right fist out in front; the heel of the right foot is up, the knees are bent, and the weight is on the left foot. (See Picture 10A)

Take a small step forward with the right foot, and lift up the left knee and fist. Pull back the right fist. (See Picture 10B) Then spring up on and kick with the right leg, hitting the foot with the extended right hand before the left foot touches down on the ground. The left fist is pulled back to the left side during the "springing up".

Now perform the exercise on the other side, substituting right for left and vice versa. Note: Do not force this movement. Practice it many times before going further. People over 40 years of age usually do not jump, but simply raise their foot and hit it with the hand. (See Picture 10C)

10A          10B          10C

# MOVEMENTS 15–32

## 15. Green Dragon Dropping Water 青龍出水

From the position shown in Picture 14, turn the left foot forward so that both feet are parallel. Pick up and place the right foot on the diagonal, with the right toes up,

the right leg straight. As you are moving the right foot, both hands shift to the right. All the weight shifts to the left foot, and the hands are positioned as shown. (See Picture 15A) (Note: This position is just like position 2D, except that the entire body faces the diagonal rather than straightforward.)

Step forward on the right foot, bring the body forward, and extend both arms. (See Picture 15B) Now bring the right foot back, with the ball of the foot touching next to the arch of the left foot, and pull the arms to the sides of the waist. (See Picture 15C) Step forward with the right foot, and bring the left foot up until the ball of the foot is touching near the arch of the right foot. Then push with the palms until the elbows are straight. (See Picture 15D)

15A

15B

15C

15D

51

# 16. Single Whip 單 鞭

16A

From the position shown in Picture 15D, move the right arm straight to the side and bend the hand down at the wrist. At the same time, bring the left arm to the chest, with the palm facing left and touching the right side of the collarbone. (See Pictures 16A-front and 16B-back) Then turn the head to the left and step out with the left foot to the left side, bending both knees and keeping the weight centered. Make sure the feet are perpendicular to each other. (See Picture 16B) Move the left hand out in a circular motion to the left until the elbow is straight and the palm is facing left. (See Picture 16C)

Note: Make sure that knees are bent, weight is centered, and arms are extended and level at shoulder height.

16B

16A-front

16B-front

16C

# 17. Wave Hands Like Clouds 擺手

Keeping the right foot fixed, step to the front with the left foot. At the same time, bring both hands to the front of the body, keeping the palms open and facing down, left hand at waist level, and right hand chest-high. (See Pictures 17A-front and 17A-back) Step sideways with the left foot while extending the right arm at shoulder-height. At the same time, bring the left arm up to chest height with the palm facing down, the fingers to the right, and the elbow forming a square angle. The head should be turned in the direction of the extended arm. (See Pictures 17B-front & 17B-back) Then swing the right arm down and around in a slow clockwise motion until it is chest high, palm down, fingers pointing to the left. At the same time, extend the left arm until it is level and straight, and bring the right foot together with the left. The head should now be turned to the left. (See Pictures 17C, 17D-front and 17D-back) Then repeat with the other arm, stepping to the left with the left foot, swinging the left arm down counter-clockwise and around, and raising the right arm. The resulting position is that in Pictures 17B-front and 17B-back. Repeat these sideways steps 6 times, always moving left, making sure to stop with the feet together as in the position shown in Picture 17C.

Note: The feet are together when the left arm is extended, but apart when the right arm is extended. The knees are always bent.

| 17D | 17C | 17B | 17A |

(Pictures are arranged right to left in order to reflect the actual movement in space.)

# 17. Wave Hands Like Clouds (continued) 擺手

17A
front view

17B

17C

17D

# 18. Single Whip　單 鞭

From the position shown in Picture 17C, move the left hand down counter-clockwise to the right side of the collarbone, palm facing left. At the same time, move the right arm straight out to the side and bend the right hand down at the wrist. (See Picture 18A) Then turn the head to the left, step out with the left foot to the left side, bending both knees, and keeping the weight centered. Make sure that the feet are perpendicular to each other. (See Pictures 18B-front and 18B-back) Move the left hand out in a circular motion to the left until the elbow is straight and the palm is facing to the left. (See Picture 18C)

18A

18B-front

18B

18C

# 19. High Pat on the Horse 高探馬

From the position shown in Picture 18c, step back with the left foot so that the toes are touching the ground in front of the right foot and both knees are bent; the body turns towards the left. The right foot turns out slightly; all the weight is on the right foot. At the same time, swing the right arm to the front so that both hands are held palms down in front of and slightly away from the body. (See Picture 19)

18C                    19

# 20. Separation of Right (Left) Foot 左右分脚

Step forward with the left foot and bring the ball of the right foot to the arch of the left foot. At the same time, bring the hands closer to the body to form an "X" with the wrists, the palms facing the body. The right hand is outside of the left hand. (See Picture 20A) Then, extend both hands out, unfolding like a fan, until they are level with the shoulders, the palms facing front. As the arms extend, kick with the right foot up in front of the right palm. (See Picture 20B)

After kicking, bring the feet back together, and retract the hands to an "X" position. In a continuous motion, extend the arms again and kick this time with the left foot. (See Picture 20C) Bring the left foot to a position in back of the right foot, with the toes touching the ground, while at the same time bringing the arms back into an "X" position in front of the chest. This "X" goes directly without pause into the next movement.

20A      20B

Note: Coordinating the extension of the arms and kicking of the foot at the same time takes approximately two years.

20C      21A

## 21. Turn Around and Kick with Sole 轉身蹬脚

With the left foot slightly behind the right foot, turn counter-clockwise 135 degrees. (See Pictures 21A and 21B) Extend the arms out level, raise the left knee to the side, then kick with the sole of the left foot. (See Pictures 21C and 21D) Then bring the left foot down with the feet wide apart and forming a "T". Bring the right arm up until it makes a triangle with the temple, and rotate the left arm down clockwise until it is slightly above and in front of the left thigh. (See Picture 21E)

21A                21B

21C                21D                21E

# 22. Wind Blowing Lotus Leaf 風擺荷葉

From the position shown in Picture 21E, turn the left foot out and then step up with the right foot next to the arch of the left foot. Straighten the left arm out level with the shoulders, palm facing forward. (See Picture 22A) Then step out diagonally with the right foot until it makes a "T" with the left foot. At the same time, the right hand pushes down in front of the body to a position over the thigh, and the left hand raises up to form a triangle with the temple. (See Picture 22B)

These movements are reversed for the other leg: turn the right foot out and step up with the left foot next to the arch of the right foot. Straighten and raise the right arm. (See Picture 22C) Then, step out diagonally with the left foot, and move the left hand down and the right hand up. (See Picture 22D) Repeat this movement six times, ending with the right hand up and the left hand down as in Picture 22D.

Note: Study the map on page 109 carefully and practice this movement for a week before going further. The hip and leg muscles may be tired for a few days because of this movement.

21E

22A

22B

22C

22D

59

## 23. Finger Block Up with Fist 指 擋 捶

From the position shown in Picture 22D, the right hand goes down to form a fist at chest level. Then, swing the left hand up until the fingers are just above the left eyebrow, with the elbow bent in a triangle. (See Picture 23A) Then punch diagonally downward with the right hand towards the left knee until the arm is straight. (See Picture 23B)

22D 23A 23B

# 24. Turn Around and Kick Two Feet Upward

翻身二起脚

24A

A. From position shown in Picture 23C, turn the toe of the left foot in about 135 degrees. At the same time, bring the left hand down to form a fist at the side of the chest. Turn the body 180 degrees clockwise and bring the right fist out in front with the fist facing up. Let the right foot slide back a few inches. Now the heel of the right foot is up, the knees are bent, and the weight is on the left foot. (See Picture 24A)

B. Take a small step forward with the right foot, lift up the left knee, and reverse the hands, extending the left fist and pulling back the right fist. (See Picture 24B) Then spring up on and kick with the right leg, hitting the foot with the extended right hand before the left foot touches down on the ground. The left hand pulls back to the left side during the "springing up". The kick then moves directly into Movement #25 without a pause.

24B

Note: Do not force this movement. Practice it many times before going further. People over 40 may not wish to jump; it is enough for them to raise their foot and hit it with the hand.

24C

## 25. Step Up, Deflect Downward, Parry and Punch

# 上步搬攔捶

After landing following the double kick, the right hand is extended and the right foot is in front. (See Picture 25A) Now make the right hand into a fist, step forward with the left foot, and open the left hand, bringing it in front of the body, the palm facing towards the body. With the right fist punch under the open left hand. (See Picture 25C)

Note: Make sure that both knees are bent and the weight centered.

25A

25B

25C

## 26. Step Back with Arms Beside Body 退步臂身

From the position shown in Picture 25b, open the right hand, step back with the right foot, and slide the left foot back with the heel up. At the same time, bend the wrists and pull both hands down to the sides of the hips. Palms are facing down, right leg is straight, and the left leg is bent. (See Picture 26A) Then, bring the arms in front to form an "X" with the left wrist over the right. (See Picture 26B)

26A         26B

## 27. Left Foot Kicks Up Forward 迎面踢脚

From the position shown in Picture 26b, open the arms up and out like a fan until they are totally extended at shoulder height with the palms facing front. Then kick forward with the left foot, with the knee straight and ankle bent. (See Picture 27A) Bring the left foot down a little in back of the right foot. At the same time, retract the hands to make an "X" across the chest, left hand inside, right hand on the outside, palms facing in. (See Picture 27B)

Note: Do not move the hands while kicking.

27A         27B

# 28. Turn and Kick With Sole 轉身蹬脚

From the position shown in Picture 27B, turn the body 270 degrees clockwise and put the body weight on the left foot as you turn. The ball of the right foot is at the arch of the left, and the heel of the right foot is up. (See Picture 28A) Extend the arms at shoulder level with palms open, raise the right knee, then kick with the right foot to the front of the right palm. (See Pictures 28B and 28C) Note that the last three kicks (Movements 24, 27 & 28) should all be on the diagonal and in the same direction.

28A        28B        28C

## 29. Step Forward, Deflect Downward, Parry and Punch

進步搬攔捶

After kicking, the right foot is extended to the right. Make the right hand into a fist (See Picture 29A), step up with the left foot until it is diagonally in front of the right (See Picture 29B), and swing the left arm around until the open left hand is over the right wrist. (See Picture 29C)

Note: Keep both knees bent and the weight in the center.

29A          29B          29C

## 30. Pull Back With Palm and Push

如封似閉

From the position shown in Picture 29C, open the right hand and pull both hands back to the chest forming a triangle. The weight is transferred to the right foot, the left knee is straight, and the left toes are up. (See Picture 30A) Push forward with both hands. The left foot is down, both knees are bent, the weight is in the center, and the hands are parallel and straight, facing the front. (See Picture 30B)

29C

30A

30B

# 31. Carry Tiger to the Mountain 抱虎歸山

From the position shown in Picture 30B, make the right hand into a fist and turn the fist upward. At the same time, put the palm of the left hand over the wrist, keeping both elbows bent. (See Picture 31A) Keeping the right foot fixed, bring the arch of the left foot to the toe of the right foot, forming a "T". (See Picture 31B) Then turn the right foot 180 degrees so that the heel of the right foot is now at the arch of the left foot. (See Picture 31C) Step up with the right foot and bring up the ball of the left foot to the arch of the right foot. (See Picture 31D).

31A          31B

31C          31D

## 32. Chop the Opponent With Fist

撇 身 捶

From the position 31D, step back diagonally with the left foot. Bend the left knee as in Exercise #5 and look to the right. As you lower down turn your right hand fist down. (See Picture 32) Note: Bend as much as possible but do not force yourself.

31D                                    32

# END OF 2ND QUARTER

| REVIEW | 15–32 Movements | One Week |
| and | | |
| PRACTICE | 1–10 Exercises | |

# BEGIN 3RD QUARTER

## Movements 33–46

# MOVEMENTS 33–46

## 33. Diagonal Single Whip 斜單鞭

Without moving the right foot, stand up and return to the position shown in Picture 31D, turning the right fist back up as you do so. (See Picture 33A) Extend the right hand outward at shoulder level, with the wrist bent downward. Bring the left arm up to the chest, making a square with the palm facing the body. (See Picture 33B) Step out to the left side with the left foot, making a "T" with both knees bent. At the same time, extend the left arm level with the shoulders, palm facing out, and turn the head to the left. (See Picture 33C)

Note: This is called the diagonal single whip. It is different from the single whip in that the left arm is brought out horizontally. Thus the left elbow begins in a higher position than for the single whip (compare Pictures 35A and 3A).

33A          33B

33C

71

## 34. Partition of the Wild Horse's Mane

野馬分鬃

Without moving the right foot, bring the ball of the left foot to the right foot arch. Make both hands into fists, and bring the right fist to the front of the right side of the chest, and the left fist to the side of the left hip. Right fist faces down but left fist faces towards your body. (See Picture 34A) Then step out diagonally with the left foot. At the same time, the right arm extends outward. (See Picture 34B) Then bring the ball of the right foot to the arch of the left foot, raise the left fist to the left side of the chest, and lower the right fist to the side of the right hip. (See Picture 34C) Now repeat the same movement on the other side, starting with the right foot. Step out with the right foot, extend the left arm, bring the left foot to the arch of the right foot, and change the fist positions. (See Pictures 34D and 34E) Do this at least seven times, ending with the right arm upraised and the left arm down (same as seen in Picture 34A).

34 right

34 left

34A

34B

34C (left side)

34D

34E

## 35. Diagonal Single Whip 斜 單 鞭

Keeping the position shown in Picture 34A, turn the body 90 degrees clockwise. Then raise the hands into the position shown in Picture 35A, and do the same diagonal single whip as described in Movement #33.

35A                    35B                    35C

## 36. Working at Shuttles Inside Clouds 雲裡穿梭

This complex movement consists of four separate punches in each direction. All four punches are identical. Study Diagram 36 carefully in order to keep the directions correct.

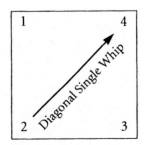

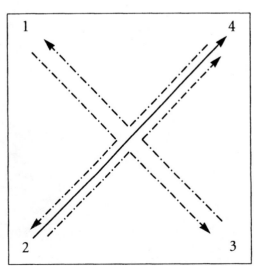

Diagram 36

# 36. Working at Shuttles Inside Clouds (continued)

雲裡穿梭

A. From the diagonal single whip (Movement #35 — left hand is pointed to corner 4 in diagram), turn the left foot inward 90 degrees. Now, bring both the right arm and leg towards the body, with the ball of the right foot touching near the left arch, and the right hand under the left elbow, palm open and facing away from the body. At the same time, the left arm also bends down with the hand formed into a fist. (See Picture 36A) Then step back with the right foot to corner 1, and turn the body 180 degrees so that it faces corner 1. While turning, pull the left fist back to the side of the body, and bring the right hand up until the open palm forms a triangle with the temple. (See turn and Picture 36B) Then punch forward with the left fist. (See Picture 36C)

36A          36 turn

36B          36C

74

# 36. Working at Shuttles Inside Clouds (continued)

雲 裡 穿 梭

B. This is a mirror image of A, except for the direction. Bring the left arm and leg towards the body, with the ball of the left foot touching near the right arch, and

simultaneously move the left hand under the right elbow, palm open and facing away from the body. At the same time, the right arm also bends down with the hand forming a fist. (See Picture 36D)

Then step out with the left foot 90 degrees to corner 2, and turn the body 90 degrees until it faces corner 2. While turning, pull the right fist back to the side of the body, and bring the left hand up until the open palm forms a triangle with the temple. (See turn and Picture 36E) Then punch with the right fist (See Picture 36F)

36D          turn

36E          36F

## 36. Working at Shuttles Inside Clouds (continued)

雲裡穿梭

C. This is identical to A, except for the direction. Turn the left foot in 90 degrees, and bring the right arm and leg towards the body, with the ball of the right foot touch-

ing next to the left foot arch, and the right hand under the left elbow, palm open and facing away from the body. At the same time, the left arm also bends down, with the hand forming a fist. (See Picture 36G) Then step with the right foot to corner 3, and turn the body until it also faces corner 3. (See turn) While turning, pull the left fist back to the side of the body, and bring the right hand up until the open palm forms a triangle with the temple. (See Picture 36H) Then punch forward with the left fist. (See Picture 36I)

36G-lift

turn

36H

36I

# 36. Working at Shuttles Inside Clouds (continued)

雲 裡 穿 梭

D. This is identical to B, except for the direction. Bring the left arm and leg towards the body, with the ball of the left foot touching near the right arch, and simultaneously move the left hand under the right elbow, palm open and facing away from the body. At the same time, the right arm also bends down with the hand forming a fist. (See Picture 36J)

Then step out with the left foot 90 degrees to corner 4, and turn the body 90 degrees until it faces corner 4. While turning, pull the right fist back to the side of the body, and bring the left hand up until the open palm forms a triangle with the temple. (See turn and Picture 36K) Then punch with the right fist. (See Picture 36L)

36J            turn

36K            36L

# 36. Working at Shuttles Inside Clouds (continued)

雲裡穿梭

36-1st corner

36-4th corner

36-2nd corner

36-3rd corner

The Four Punches

## 37. Step Up and Grasp Bird's Tail

轉身攬雀尾

According to the floor diagram, this movement continues along the diagonal line from corner 2 to corner 4. (See Diagram 36) From the last position of Movement 36, bring the right foot up until the ball of the foot touches next to the arch of the left foot; right heel is up. At the same time, move both hands down until the palms are below waist level and facing each other. (See Picture 37A) Step forward along the diagonal with the right foot and extend both arms, right palm facing down, left palm facing up, both elbows straight. (See Picture 37B) Then slide both hands down to left side of body at hip level, and shift the body weight back until the right knee is straight with right toes up; the left knee is bent. Both elbows are bent, left palm is up, and right palm is down. (See Picture 37C) Bring hands up simultaneously, and step forward with left foot until the ball of the foot is touching next to the arch of the right foot, keeping left heel up. (See Picture 37D) Then push with both hands along diagonal line towards corner 4. (See Picture 37E)

36L

37A

37B

37C

37D

37E

# 38. Single Whip　單　鞭

From the position shown in Picture 37E, pivot both feet slightly to the left. Move the right arm straight to the side, bending the right hand down at the wrist. At the same time, bring the left arm to the chest, with the palm facing left and touching right side of the collarbone. Then do the "single whip" movement as described and shown in Movement 16: turn the head to the left, step out with the left foot to the left side, bending both knees and keeping the weight centered. Make sure that the feet are perpendicular to each other. Move the left hand out in a circular motion to the left until the elbow is straight and the palm is facing left. (See Pictures 38A, 38B and 38C)

38A　　　　　　　　38B　　　　　　　　38C

# 39. Wave Hands Like Clouds　擺　手

Upon finishing Movement 38, proceed to "wave hands like clouds" as in Movement 17: keeping the right foot fixed, step to the front with the left foot. At the same time, bring both hands to the front of the body, keeping the palms open and facing down, left hand at waist level, and right hand chest-high. (See Pictures 39A-front and 39A-back) Step sideways with the left foot while extending the right arm at shoulder height. At the same time, bring the left arm up to chest height, with the palm down, the fingers pointing to the right, and the elbow forming a square angle. The head should be turned in the direction of the extended arm. (See Pictures 39B-front and 39B-back) Then swing the right arm down and around in a slow clockwise motion until it is chest-high and pointing to the left. At the same time, extend the left arm until it is level and straight, and bring the right foot together with the left. The head should now be turned to the left. (See Pictures 39C-front and 39C-back) Then repeat with the other arm, stepping to the left with the left foot, swinging the left arm down counter-clockwise and around and raising the right arm. The resulting position is that in Pictures 39B-front and 39B-back. Repeat these sideways steps only two times, always moving left, making sure to stop with the feet together as shown in Picture 39C.

Note: The feet are together when the left arm is extended, but apart when the right arm is extended. The knees are always bent.

(Pictures are arranged right to left in order to reflect the actual movement in space.)

| 39D | 39C | 39B | 39A |

| 39A-front | 39B | 39C | 39D |

## 40. Single Whip Lowering Down 單 鞭 下 勢

From the position shown in Picture 39C, move the left hand down counter-clockwise to the collarbone, palm facing left; and at the same time, move the right arm straight to the right side and bend the hand down at the wrist. Now do a "single whip" as described and shown in Movement 18. Upon completing the single whip (see Picture 40A), turn the left toe inward 90 degrees and bend down as in Exercise 5: the right knee is bent, and the body is turned to the left side. Keep the arms extended straight, with the left palm facing out, and the right palm facing up and fingers pointing up. (See Pictures 40B and 40C)

40A

Note: Remember that this is an extremely difficult movement and requires years to perfect. It is very important to practice the movement properly: keep the feet parallel and flat on the ground; keep the left leg straight; the hips are rotated towards the right but the shoulders are in line with the left leg.

40B

40C

## 41. Golden Cock Stands on One Leg 金 鶏 獨 立

Stand up, turning the left toe towards the front and bringing the left hand down to the left hip, with palm facing down. Keep the right hand extended as before, left knee bent, and right leg extended back and straight. (See Picture 41A) Pull the right leg up and forward, while at the same time sliding the right hand along the top of thigh to knee. (See Picture 41B) Then raise the hand back towards the side of chest, palm facing forward. (See Picture 41C). Kick out the heel of right leg and push forward with palm of right hand until both leg and arm are extended. (See Picture 41D) Step forward by bringing the right leg down and at the same time turn the right palm up and bring the right hand to the right side of hip. After the right foot steps down, raise the left leg up and forward, and repeat the same steps by extending the left leg and arm. (See the sequence 41E, 41F, 41G & 41H) Repeat these steps from 6 to 12 times, stopping with the left foot extended.

41A   41B   41C   41D

41E   41F   41G   41H

# 42. Step Back and Repulse Monkey 倒攆猴

First Part: From the final position as shown in Picture 41g, lower the extended left foot until the heel touches the ground. The left hand is extended in front with the palm facing out; the right hand is at the right side of the hip with the palm facing up. (See Picture 42A) Then "step back and repulse monkey" as described and shown in Movement 10: the left knee is straight, the left toes up, and the right knee bent; the shoulders and hips are straight.

Second Part: Turn left palm up, at the same time raise the right hand to the chest and turn the right palm facing front. (See Picture 41B) Step back with the left foot and bring the left hand to the left side of the hip while pushing forward with the right hand. The right knee and the right arm are straight and the right toes are up. (See Picture 42C)

Third Part: (This is a mirror image of the second part.) Turn the right palm up; at the same time raise the left hand up to the chest and turn the palm facing front. (See Picture 42D) Step back with the right foot and bring the right hand to the right side of the hip while

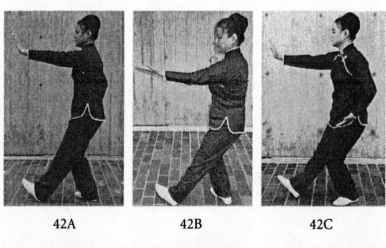

| 42A | 42B | 42C |

| 42D | 42E | 42F | 42G |

pushing forward with the left hand. The left knee and arm are straight and the left toes are up. (See Picture 42E) Alternate the second and third parts three times each, ending with the right arm extended. (See Picture 42F)

Note: The right palm faces up at the beginning of this movement, unlike at the beginning of Movement 10.

# 43. Slow Palm Slanting Flying 挫掌斜飛

From the position of Movement 42G, bring the right foot back until the ball of the foot is next to the arch of the left foot, with the heel up. At the same time, put wrists together making an "X", with right hand below facing up, and left hand above facing down. Keep both elbows slightly bent. (See Picture 43A)

Step forward diagonally 45 degrees, and at the same time, turn right palm so that it faces the body. Spread out the hands, and bring them up to the shoulders like a bird spreading its wings. Keep the elbows straight and the right hand slightly higher than the left hand, both palms facing back. Shoulders are down, hips and shoulders are straight to the body, and head is facing right. (See Pictures 43B and 43C)

Note: Make sure both knees are bent and weight is in the middle. Right hand should be in line with the right foot, and left hand in line with the middle of the left foot.

43A

43B

43C

## 44. Raise Right (Left) Hand 左右提手

Raise Right Hand: From the position shown in Picture 43C, keep the right foot stationary and step forward with the left foot, keeping the toes up and the knee straight. Bring both hands to the front, right hand closer to the body and facing the left elbow. Keep both elbows bent. (See Picture 44A) Take a small step forward with the left foot, and at the same time, bring the ball of the right foot next to the arch of the left foot, keeping the heel up. All the weight is on the left foot. Bring both hands together, brushing the palm of the left hand with the back of the right hand. (See Picture 44B) Continue raising the right hand until it is straight at shoulder level with palm facing down, and bring the left hand to the waist with palm up. (See Picture 44C) Step back with the right foot, and bring the hands back to the original position. (See Picture 44A)

Raise Left Hand: Now turn the body to the right 180 degrees, bringing the right toes up and the right arm out, farther than the left. The body is now a mirror image of Picture 44a. (See Picture 44D) In the reverse of the first part, raise the left hand straight up to shoulder height, brushing past the right palm as the right hand is brought down to the front of the waist. (See Picture 44E) Step back, and at the same time, bring the left hand past the right hand back to the beginning position shown in Picture 44D. The right toes are up and the right knee is straight.

Note: Make sure the shoulders are straight.

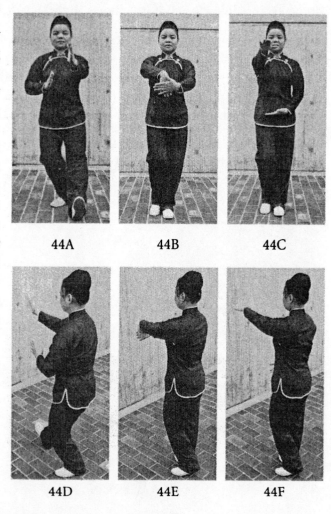

44A      44B      44C

44D      44E      44F

# 45. Fly Pulling Back and Step Up 飛 櫊 上 勢

From position shown in Picture 44D, step forward slightly with the right foot, while extending both arms until the elbows are straight, with right palm down and left palm up. (See Picture 45A) Step back with right foot, bringing the ball of the right foot next to the arch of the left foot. At the same time, bring both hands back with right forearm across the waist, and the palm facing the body. The left palm is at the left hip facing the right hand. (See Picture 45B) Step forward with right foot, then bring up left foot until the ball of the left foot is next to the arch of the right foot. Raise the right arm to the chest, palm down, while keeping left hand at the side. (See Picture 45C)

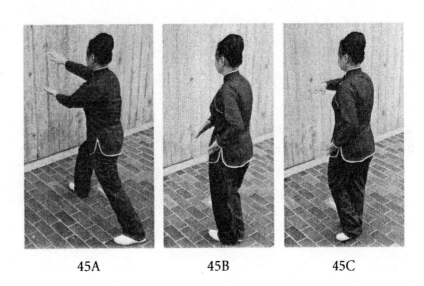

45A          45B          45C

## 46. Fan Through the Arm 扇 通 臂

Now turn face to the left and step to the left side with the left foot. Bend both knees and keep weight in the center. The left toe is pointing left forming a "T" to the right foot. (See Picture 46A) Moving both hands at the same time, bring the left arm up until it is straight from the shoulder with palm facing front, and bring the right hand back to the right side of the shoulder, palm facing front. (See Pictures 46B front and back)

| 46A | 46B | 46B- front |

# END OF 3RD QUARTER

REVIEW      33 – 46 Movements       Break one week
and
PRACTICE    Double Kick Exercises, #5, #4

# BEGIN 4TH QUARTER

## Movements 47–64

# MOVEMENTS 47–64

## 47. Strike Opponent's Ears with Both Fists 雙風貫耳

From the last position of "fan through the arm," turn the left toes out towards the front, and then step forward with the right foot. Push with both palms open towards the left side, until the left arm is bent square at the elbow and the right arm bent only at the wrist. Both knees are bent with the weight on the left foot, and the right foot rests on its ball, heel slightly up. (See Picture 47A) Next, move both hands to the front of the chest. (See Picture 47B) Step forward with the right foot, followed

by the left foot, and push directly forward with both hands until the elbows are straight. Both knees are bent, the left foot is few inches behind and diagonal to the right foot, which is pointed straight. Both feet are flat on the ground. (See Picture 47C) Now make fists of both hands. (See Picture 47D) Step forward with the right foot, followed by the left, and at the same time bring the two fists together until they are almost touching. Both feet are flat on the ground, left foot a few inches behind the right, and both knees bent.

46B

47A

47B

47C

47D

# 48. Through Sky Cannon 通天炮

From the position shown in Picture 47D, step forward with the right foot, followed by the left. Both feet are flat on the ground, knees bent, and left foot is a few inches behind the right. At the same time turn both fists up and bend the elbows slightly. The left fist should be slightly lower and at the height of the right wrist. (See Picture 48)

Note: Do not hold the fists too tightly.

47D                48

# 49. Single Whip 單 鞭

From the last position as shown in Picture 48, pivot the right foot around 90 degrees, and place the ball of the left foot near the arch of the right foot. At the same time, extend and rotate the right arm so that the right hand is bent down at the wrist, and bring the left hand back to the chest. (See Picture 49A) Then do the "single whip" as described and shown in Movement 3: turn the head to the left, step out with the left foot to the left side, bending both knees and keeping the weight centered. Make sure that the feet are perpendicular to each other. Move the left hand out in a circular motion to the left side until the elbow is straight and the palm is facing left. (See Pictures 49B and 49C)

49A           49B           49C

# 50. Wave Hands Like Clouds 擺 手

Upon finishing the "single whip," proceed to "wave hands like clouds" as in Movement 17, although this time you are facing the opposite direction. Keeping the right foot fixed, step to the front with the left foot. At the same time, bring both hands to the front of the body, keeping the palms open and facing down, left hand at waist level, and right hand chest-high. (See Pictures 50A-front & 50A-back) Step sideways with the left foot while extending the right arm. At the same time, bring the left arm up to chest height with the palm down, fingers pointing to the right, and the elbow forming a square. The head should be turned in the direction of the extended arm. (See Pictures 50B-front and 50B-back) Then swing the right arm down and around in a slow clockwise motion until it is chest-high and pointing to the left. At the same time, extend the left arm until it is level and straight, and bring the right foot together with the left. The head should now be turned to the left. (See Pictures 50C-front & 50C-back) Then repeat with the other arm, stepping to the left with the left foot, swinging the left arm down counter-clockwise and around, and raising the right arm. The resulting position is that in Pictures 50B-front and back. Repeat these sideway steps 4 times, always moving left, making sure to stop with the feet together as shown in Picture 50C.

Note: The feet are together when the left arm is extended, but apart when the right arm is extended. The knees are always bent.

(Pictures are arranged right to left in order to reflect the actual movement in space.)

| 50D | 50C | 50B | 50A |

| 50A-front | 50B | 50C | 50D |

## 51. Single Whip  單 鞭

From position shown in 50C, bring arms into position for executing "single whip": left hand comes back to rest in front of right side of the collarbone, palm facing left, while right arm swings back to right side, hand bent down at wrist. (See Picture 51A) Step out with left foot to left side. Move left hand out in circular motion to left side until the elbow is straight and palm faces left. (See Picture 51B)

51A         51B         51C

## 52. High Pat on the Horse

高 探 馬

From position shown in Picture 51B, step back with the left foot so that the ball of the foot is touching the ground in front of the right foot and both knees are bent; the body turns towards the left. The right foot is turned slightly out, all the weight resting on the right foot. At the same time, swing the right arm to the front so that both hands are held palms down in front of and slightly away from the body at shoulder height. (See Picture 52)

52

## 53. Cross Wave of Water Lily 十字擺蓮

From the position of "high pat on horse," take a step diagonally with the left foot, keeping both knees bent and moving the hands to keep them centered in front of the chest. (See Picture 53A) Swing the right foot in an arch clockwise in front of the body, slapping the palms of both hands with the right side of the right foot. After kicking, return to the same position. (See Pictures 53B, 53C)

53A       53B       53C

## 54. Downward Fist 栽　捶

Make the right hand into a fist and bring the left hand up to the left eyebrow, forming a triangle with the head. At the same time, punch with the right fist directly downward. Keep the weight in the middle and the back straight. (See Pictures 54A and 54B)

54A       54B

## 55. Step Up and Grasp Bird's Tail

# 上步攬雀尾

As in Movement 37, bring the right foot up until the ball of the foot touches next to the arch of the left foot; right heel is up. At the same time, move both hands down until the palms are below waist level and facing each other. (See Picture 55A) Step forward along the diagonal with the right foot and extend both arms, right palm facing down, left palm facing up, and both elbows straight. (See Picture 55B) Then slide both hands down to the left side of body

55A

at hip level, and shift the body weight back until the right knee is straight with right toes up; the left knee is bent. Both elbows are bent, left palm is up and right palm is down. (See Picture 55C) Bring hands up simultaneously, and step forward with the ball of the left foot next to the right foot arch, keeping the left heel up. Then push with both hands along diagonal line away from body. (See Picture 55D)

55B

55C

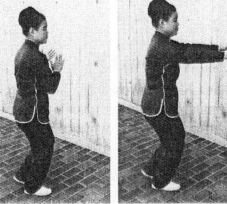

55D                    55E

97

## 56. Single Whip　　單　鞭

From the position shown in Picture 55D, pivot both feet slightly to the left. Move the right arm straight to the side, bending the right hand down at the wrist. At the same time, bring the left arm to the chest, with the palm facing left and touching right side of the collarbone. Then do the "single whip" movement as described and shown in Movement 16: turn the head to the left, step out with the left foot to the left side, bending both knees and keeping the weight centered. Make sure that the feet are perpendicular to each other. Move the left hand out in a circular motion to the left until the elbow is straight and the palm is facing left. (See Pictures 56A, 56B and 56C)

56A　　　　　　　　　　56B　　　　　　　　　　56C

## 57. Wave Hands Like Clouds　　擺　手

Upon finishing Movement 56, proceed to "wave hands like clouds" as in Movement 17: keeping the right foot fixed, step to the front with the left foot. At the same time, bring both hands to the front of the body, keeping the palms open and facing down, left hand at waist level, and right hand chest-high. (See Pictures 57A-front and 57A-back) Step sideways with the left foot while extending the right arm. At the same time, bring the left arm up to chest-height with the palm down, fingers pointing to the right, and the elbow forming a square. The head should be turned in the direction of the extended arm. (See Pictures 57B-front & 57B-back) Then swing the right arm down and around in a slow clockwise motion until it is chest high and pointing to the left. At the same time, extend the left arm until it is level and straight, and bring the right foot together with the left. The head should now be turned to the left. (See Pictures 57C-front and 57C-back) Then repeat with the other arm, stepping to the left with the left foot, swinging the left arm down counter-clockwise and around, and raising the right arm. The resulting position is that in Pictures 57B-front and 57B-back. Repeat these sideway steps 4 times, always moving left, making sure to stop with the feet together as is shown in Picture 57C.

Note: The feet are together when the left arm is extended, but apart when the right arm is extended. The knees are always bent.

(Pictures are arranged right to left in order to reflect the actual movement in space.)

57D       57C       57B       57A

57A-front       57B       57C       57D

# 58. Single Whip Lowering Down 單鞭下勢

From the position shown in Picture 57C, move the left hand down counter-clockwise to the collarbone, palm facing left; and at the same time, move the right arm straight to the side and bend the hand down at the wrist.

Now do a "single whip" movement as described in Movement 18. Upon completing the single whip (See Picture 58A), turn the left toe inward 90 degrees and bend down as in Exercise 5: the right knee is bent, and the body is turned to the left side. Keep the arms extended straight, with the left palm facing out, and the right palm facing up and fingers pointing up. (See Picture 58B)

58A

58B

58B front view

## 59. Step Up to Form Seven Stars 上步七星

From the last position of "single whip lowering down," turn the left foot out and form a fist in the right hand. Stand up on the left foot, bringing the right foot 3 inches behind and slightly to the side of the left heel. Bend down on both knees, and punch forward with the right fist until the elbow is straight. While punching with the right fist, bring the left hand back so that the left arm is bent and the left

59A                    59B

palm faces the right wrist. (See Pictures 59A and 59B) The right heel is up, the back is straight.

## 60. Retreat to Ride Tiger 退步跨虎

From the position shown in Picture 59B, stand up by stepping back with the right foot. At the same time, swing back with the right hand and swing the left hand forward. The right fist opens up during the backwards swinging motion. Right palm is facing up and left palm is facing right. (See Picture 60A)

Now step cross-wise to the right with the left foot, keeping the left heel up and turning the body 90 degrees clockwise. Body weight moves to the right foot. At the same time, swing the right arm to the front and the left arm to the back. (See Picture 60B) Keep both knees bent. The right palm, extended in front of the chest, is facing out front; keep left wrist straight and palm facing up.

60A                    60B

## 61. Slanting Body and Turn the Moon

斜 身 扭 月

From the position shown in Picture 60B, pivot the body 180 degrees in a clockwise direction, without moving the relative position of the arms or legs. Step diagonally to the left with left foot, keeping both knees bent, shoulders and hips straight. (See Pictures 61A and 61B)

61A

61B-front

61B-side view

## 62. Wave Lotus Foot　擺　蓮　脚

From the position shown in Picture 61B, extend the left
hand to front of body next to right hand and, at the same
time, kick with the right leg clockwise, slapping both
~~ght side of the foot.~~
~~ut leave both hands~~
(See Picture 62)

62

**d Arrow　彎 弓 射 虎**

s with both
in small cir-
cles in front of the body: left fist clockwise, right
fist counter-clockwise. Start first with the right
hand, and make three rotations with hands before
stopping. (See Picture 63)

63

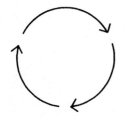

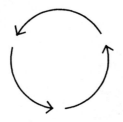

103

# 64. Right Grasp Bird's Tail 左右攬雀尾

From the position shown in Picture 63, step forward with the ball of the right foot to the arch of the left foot. Move both fists down just in front of waist. (See Picture 64A) Then step out diagonally with the right foot, shifting weight accordingly, and extend both arms in the same diagonal direction, with left palm facing up and right palm facing down. (See Picture 64B) Then slide both hands down to waist-level on the left side, shifting the weight back to the left leg. Left knee is bent, right knee is straight, and right toes are up. Both hands are waist high above the left knee, and both elbows are bent. (See Picture 64C) Lean forward to shift weight to middle and bend both knees. Raise both hands past the chest (see Picture 64D) and push them diagonally to the right side until they are fully extended. (See Picture 64E) Then move the right foot back until the ball of the foot is at the left foot arch and bring both hands back to front of waist as shown in Picture 64A.

64-right          64-left

# 64. Right Grasp Bird's Tail (continued) 左右攬雀尾

64A        64B        64C

64D        64E        64F

# 64. Left Grasp Bird's Tail 左右覽雀尾

From Position 64A step back diagonally with the right foot. At the same time extend both arms diagonally to the left side with the right palm facing up and the left palm down. (See Picture 64B-left) Then slide hands down to waist level on the right side, shifting body weight accordingly, with left knee straight, toes up, and right knee bent. (See Picture 64C-left) Now raise both hands past the chest (see Picture 64D-left) and push them diagonally to the left until fully extended; palms are turned up at wrists, as shown in Picture 64e. Weight is in the middle with both knees bent. Then turn both palms up and make an "X" with left palm on top and right underneath. (See Picture 64F) Step back with the left foot, and bring both hands to the waist. (See Picture 64G) Stand straight with knees together. Uncross the hands, and extend both arms sideways to shoulder height. (See Picture 64H) Move both hands up to eyebrows, forming triangles. (See Picture 64I) Push with both palms straight down and then pull hands to the sides next to the hips. (See Picture 64J) Then straighten both hands, letting them fall next to the body. (See Picture 64K)

64A-left

64B-left

64C-left

64D-left

# Conclusion of Grand Terminus 合太極

64E         64F         64G

64H         64I         64J

64K

學生們請記住

一日練一日功

一日不練十日鬆

臥拳練前 慢練鬆

不緊不慢練成功！

郭連蔭田言

To My Students:
Practice, Practice Everyday
Miss One Day Lose Ten Days
No Hurry No Slack
A Well-Paced Practice
Is The Way To Success
from Sifu Kuo Lien-Ying

# Tai-Chi Chuan's 64 Stances as Taught by Kuo Lien-Ying
## Chart for Advanced Students

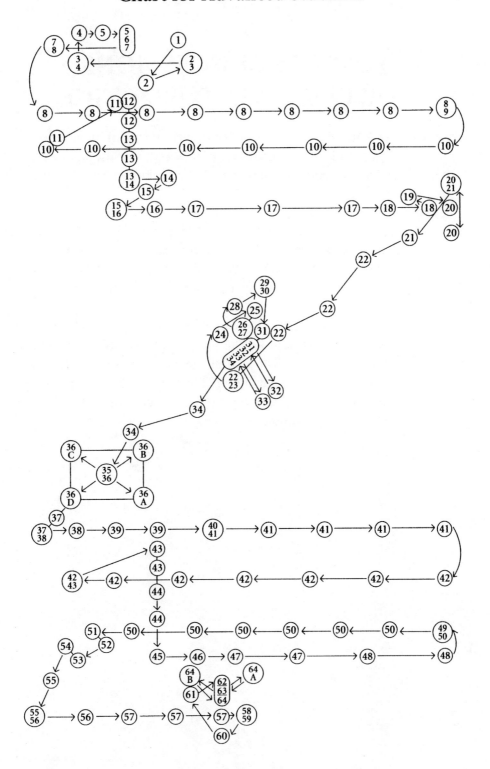

# FURTHER SUGGESTIONS
# FOR CONTINUED PRACTICE

Once you have learned a certain series of movements, you must repeat and carefully study each of them in order to understand fully the significance of each one. This habit of practice not only makes for better exercise but also aids in cultivating a fine technique.

Every movement in Tai-Chi Chuan involves the entire body; the parts of the body move in unison and therefore develop evenly. During your first year, you may not always achieve this harmony and thereby may neglect certain parts of the body. When you practice, you must be sure to exercise the entire body so as to develop the special beauty and grace of the circular movements.

Although you may be physically weak when you begin, or you may seem to be a slow learner, you should not be discouraged. Think about old sayings like "hard work never fails" and "after the bitter comes the sweet" when your efforts do not seem to be paying off. The truth is that every effort you make in practicing Tai-Chi Chuan does pay off eventually. As long as you persevere, good results will follow.

# IMPORTANT NOTES
# TO REMEMBER WHEN PRACTICING

1. Positions should be correct and accurate; the mind must be concentrated.

2. Actions should be harmonious, with attention focused solely on Tai-Chi Chuan.

3. Advance and retreat should be easily interchangeable, and *hsu* and *shih* clearly differentiated.

4. Front and back should be connected, and up and down inter-related.

5. Speed of movements should be even, and the breathing natural.

Although these five points may seem brief, they are the most basic rules of Tai-Chi Chuan and must be faithfully carried out. They also represent the basic standards by which the practice of Tai-Chi Chuan is judged.

# III

# AN INTRODUCTION TO THE MAJOR CONCEPTS OF TAI-CHI CHUAN

This section presents the concepts that are central to the meaning of Tai-Chi Chuan. You might want to re-read these explanations at regular intervals over the course of your study of Tai-Chi Chuan. Your understanding of each concept will grow and develop as your body learns the lessons of the physical exercises. And you may feel a sense of achievement as your knowledge deepens with each successive reading.

The Major Concepts:

*Hsu* and *Shih*
"Thought" and "Strength"
"Lightness" and "Nimbleness"
Correct Posture
"Coordination"
"Stillness"
*Tan-tien*
*Din-jin*

## The Concepts of *Hsu* and *Shih*

Shih, the positive, means substantial and solid; not stagnant, stiff, or deadened. Therefore, positive actions should be measured and careful. Hsu, the negative, means spontaneous, lively, and spirited; negative actions demand flexibility and easy movement. In Tai-Chi Chuan, you must learn to understand hsu and shih and the relationship between them, which is dynamic and constantly changing. Shih prepares for hsu; hsu prepares for shih.

In terms of the lower body, if your left leg is supporting the major part of your weight, your left leg is considered positive. When the weight of your body is shifted to the right leg, then your right leg becomes positive while your left leg becomes negative. Whenever a leg is in the positive position, it

113

must support the weight of your body without wavering. Whenever a leg is in the negative position, it must be able to be moved easily.

The concepts of *shih* and *hsu* are particularly helpful in the development of lower body strength. Normally, both legs support the weight of the body, but in Tai-Chi Chuan your weight is supported by one leg at a time so that each leg must independently be as strong as both legs together. The demand on each leg therefore is at least twice as great in Tai-Chi Chuan as in other exercises.

The warm-up stretching exercises are important for developing the flexibility needed for learning *shih* and *hsu*. During practice of the Tai-Chi Chuan set, you should pay special attention to *shih* and *hsu* when doing a turn or a T-stance. Distinguishing between the positive and negative leg makes it much easier to maintain your balance while turning. And in the T-stance, your awareness of *shih* and *hsu* will help you to keep your positive leg firm and steady while you move your negative leg lightly, without apparent effort.

When practicing Tai-Chi Chuan in line with the principles of *shih* and *hsu*, you should also pay attention to the distance between steps and the firmness of each step you take. Tai-Chi Chuan steps should not be too small nor too far apart. If the distance between the legs is too great, you will not be able to change positions with nimble steps. This will deaden the spirit of the whole exercise. Yet your movements must also be firm and powerful. This means that you should move with strength and agility, like a cat.

As your weight shifts from one leg to the other, your lower body constantly changes its *hsu* and *shih* qualities. Even in those movements where it is not easy to distinguish *shih* from *hsu*, you must concentrate on determining which leg is positive or negative. The concept of "dual strength", which means that the weight of the body is resting equally on both legs, does not apply to Tai-Chi Chuan, although it is used in other martial arts such as Shao-Lin Chuan. If you are not aware of *shih* and *hsu*, your Tai-Chi Chuan movements become clumsy, and the benefits of the physical exercise are diminished.

Thus far, the concepts of *shih* and *hsu* have been described in relation to the lower body. However, in Tai-Chi Chuan you must also distinguish between them in the upper body: in the trunk, in the arms and hands, and in fact, in every part of the body. The traditional saying — "everywhere there is a *shih* and a *hsu*"— is simply the expression of this idea and one of the central features of Tai-Chi Chuan.

Although the concepts of positive and negative are easier to grasp in reference to the lower body, you can distinguish them in the upper body if you use the concept of "thought" or concentration. This means that whichever part of the body you are concentrating on becomes the positive; and those areas of the body that you are not thinking about are considered the negative. For example, in the single whip, the left hand is the positive element because at this time the mind is concentrating on the left hand. This is the first step in distinguishing between *shih* and *hsu* in the single whip. The second step involves concentrating on the left hand itself: the outside of the left hand is considered positive, the inside negative. Therefore, in the single whip movement, there is a clear division between *shih* and *hsu* which becomes further refined as the concentration deepens.

Students must be aware, however, that *shih* and *hsu* are dynamic; they vary with changes in position and last only short lengths of time in different parts of the body. They change according to the changes in the positions of the Tai-Chi Chuan movements. As it is written in the *Tai-Chi Chuan Dictionary* by Wang Tsung-Yue of the Ching Dynasty, "The left is positive; it then becomes negative . . . the right is heavy; it then becomes light."

The crucial step towards achieving complete understanding of *shih* and *hsu* in all parts of the body is the ability to perceive the subtle changing and shifting of the *shih* and *hsu* elements. It requires a long period of practice, as it is definitely not an easy task. Keep the following points in mind as you attempt to master the *shih* and *hsu* concepts:

1. In every movement you should distinguish the *shih* and *hsu* of the LOWER body first.

2. Then, you should use "thought," and learn which part of the body you should concentrate on for each movement. Eventually, you should attempt to apply the use of "thought" in all parts of the body.

3. You should not practice too fast but should aim for complete mastery. After you study Tai-Chi Chuan for three years, you can then practice pushing hands. At that time you will learn how to distinguish the changes in *shih* and *hsu* as they relate to the meaning of force. When your hands are able to do what the mind intends for them to do, then you can be considered accomplished.

## The Concepts of "Thought" and "Strength"

In Tai-Chi Chuan the emphasis is placed on "thought" or mental concentration rather than on "strength" or physical force. Tai-Chi Chuan movements demand naturalness; they should not be forced. Physical force or "strength" should not be exerted to stop or start the contraction of the body muscles for any movements. For example, when you make a fist, your hand should not be squeezed tightly. When you strike out, you should not strike blindly or wildly. In kicking, lift the foot gradually, and then kick out slowly and lightly without using "strength." Direct your mind to concentrate on each movement.

Although all physical exercise helps the circulation of the blood and strengthens the heart, many believe that if muscles are over-exerted, circulation may be obstructed. Since Tai-Chi Chuan movements are neither fast nor slow and are governed by "thought" rather than "strength," Tai-Chi Chuan is well suited for improving blood circulation. You should seek to concentrate closely on the sequence of moves. When performing the single whip, for example, your "thought" should pass from the right hand, through the shoulders, to the left hand. This encourages the blood to flow from the right hand through the shoulder, to the heart, and finally to the left arm and hand. As a result, when the left hand is extended, the fingertips will seem to expand, and they will tingle and feel warm. In Tai-Chi Chuan, this is called the achievement of "thought."

Another benefit of using "thought" is that your mental functions will also be improved. Some Tai-Chi Chuan movements are complex and require great concentration; therefore many believe that they help to train the central nervous system.

## The Concepts of "Lightness" and "Nimbleness"

The concept of "thought" or mental concentration requires that your movements be lively yet smooth. In Tai-Chi Chuan this is known as "lightness" and "nimbleness" and refers to the relaxation of all muscles during the exercises. If muscles are taut, your entire body becomes tight, and your bones come under pressure and become brittle. When you achieve "lightness" and "nimbleness" your tendons stretch, which permits your bones to develop tensile strength. Blood circulation is also improved.

For beginning students, "lightness" and "nimbleness" are difficult to achieve because normally in the human body there is always some tension. Even when practicing Tai-Chi Chuan, there is a tendency for the body to become tense after you do a few movements; therefore, you must pay special attention to relaxing the muscles as you move. It will be helpful at first to try to relax mentally, while repeating the traditional saying — "Use thought, not strength."

For the advanced student, pushing hands with a partner is a lively and spirited exercise for learning the further meaning of "lightness" and "nimbleness." When your muscles are relaxed and your movements are fluid, it is easier for you to defend against the attacks of your opponent and adapt to his actions.

## The Concepts Involved in Correct Posture

When you are practicing and begin to feel uncomfortable you should check your posture. In Tai-Chi Chuan correct posture means a certain way of bearing your body and limbs based on two key concepts: "central spine" and "comfort and ease of center." You should pay careful attention to keeping your coccyx (the small bone at the base of your spinal column) in a central position. This prevents falling forward or backward or leaning to the left or right. However, you should NOT make any unnecessary effort to straighten the spinal column: "central spine" means a natural central equilibrium. Achieving the "comfort and ease of the center" means that the equilibrium should be maintained with relaxed muscles. Thus, in order to be balanced, correct posture involves both equilibrium and relaxation.

Correct posture also demands that you "loosen the pelvic muscles." The muscles of the pelvis are linked with the skeleton, and when they are tightened, the muscles of the limbs will also tighten. Thus, any tension of the "pelvic" muscles will stiffen your movement. When there is no tension in the pelvic region, all bone joints are loose and all muscles relaxed, so you can move your limbs freely. Therefore you should try to avoid tension in the waist and pelvic area. Then you will have no difficulty in achieving beneficial changes from the mental and physical exercises.

It should be emphasized that relaxing the pelvic region helps especially in the development of mental force, which is the central feature of Tai-Chi Chuan. To quote Master Kuo Lien-Ying, "Consciousness commences in the waist because the waist controls the entire body." With loose and flexible pelvic muscles you can control all parts of your body and develop mental strength with ease. "Loosening the pelvic muscles" should not be misunderstood to mean a completely relaxed and thereby weakened waist area: the strength of Tai-Chi Chuan is a combination of hard and soft energy, and there should be — alternately — relaxation and tension. (Note: Pay particular attention to relaxing the pelvic region in the following movements: brush knee twist; step up and push; deflect downward, parry and punch; fan through the arm; single whip lowering down; and raise right and left hand.)

In a correct posture, you must keep all of these points in mind. Remember that you should not do one thing to the neglect of the others.

# The Concept of "Coordination"

In the art of Tai-Chi Chuan, the movement of all parts of the body in harmony is "coordination." It cannot be learned, however, without first learning balance. According to Master Kuo Lien-Ying, "The Tai-Chi Chuan exercise has its roots in the feet, is controlled by the waist and is expressed by the fingers." The movement upward from the feet through the legs to the waist demands "coordination." Therefore you must treat all parts of the body together as a whole when you practice any movement. Consider, for example, that your feet are like the roots of a plant and they provide stability for the body. Or that your waist is the focal point, the center of all bodily movement. The strength that radiates from the waist descends through the legs to the feet, and ascends through the shoulders to the arms and hands. Every movement involves the whole body, and this is the basis of "coordination."

How is good coordination achieved? During the practice of Tai-Chi Chuan your hands and feet must move simultaneously. At the beginning, students should watch out for the common mistake of moving their feet before their hands. For example, in the Step Back and Repulse the Monkey movement, your right hand and right foot must be extended at the same time; likewise the left hand should be moved with the left foot. Another common problem lies in students' inability to bend the knees and keep the waist flexible at the same time. The waist and legs are critical in the "coordination" of the body; according to Master Kuo, the cause of any confusion of movement is to be found either in the waist or the legs. The waist must act as the pivotal point so that "coordination" will be achieved.

For more advanced students, pushing hands can further develop the "coordination" of the hands with the simultaneous movement of the rest of the body. If you fail to observe the rule — when your opponent moves backward, you push, and when he moves forward, you yield — you will certainly lose balance and "coordination" will be lost.

# The Concept of "Stillness"

In the practice of Tai-Chi Chuan you must develop a calm spirit and a tranquil heart, as well as smooth, flowing movements. This evenness of spirit is called "stillness" and refers both to the physical or physiological processes and to the processes of the mind. Since, however, it is true that there is never absolute stillness in the universe, not on the atomic or the cosmic levels, what is asked of a Tai-Chi Chuan student is that he or she develop relative "stillness."

The physical aspect of "stillness" involves slow and gentle motions of the body. Respiration is deep and long; the heart is slow and steady; the circulation of the blood is even and smooth. After a long period of study, the "stillness" of Tai-Chi Chuan brings peace to an anxious and troubled mind.

While practicing, you must think of nothing but the movement itself. At the same time, you must be able to keep your eyes open and not see the external world; to hear, but not listen. During intensive exercise, you are quiet and calm. Only with the daily cultivation of the movements will you truly understand the meaning of "stillness.

## The Concept of *Tan-Tien*

The term *tan-tien,* as used by the Taoists and as found in ancient Chinese medical treatises, designates a region within the abdomen, slightly below the navel. It is not, however, to be identified as a specific anatomical structure within the abdominal cavity. *Tan-tien* can also be understood as a type of natural breathing in which the lower abdomen is slightly extended by the descending action of the diaphragm muscle. This form of breathing, through the massaging action of the diaphragm, serves to stimulate and tone the abdominal organs and nerve networks, as well as to increase the efficiency of the lungs, to improve the circulation of the blood, and to strengthen the abdominal muscles themselves.

You should practice this method of natural breathing frequently. While doing Tai-Chi Chuan you must "let the *chi* sink to the *tan-tien,*"[1] as Wang Tsung-Yue taught in his classic text. It is the mind that must be used in directing the *chi,* not muscular force. By doing the exercises repeatedly and with the correct attitude, the *chi* will automatically sink to the *tan-tien.* You must not daydream nor be occupied by any thoughts while practicing Tai-Chi Chuan. This implies constant alertness and centeredness. The practice of *tan-tien* breathing will, in effect, clear and refresh the mind. You should practice this until it becomes totally in harmony with the movements of Tai-Chi Chuan. With the center in the *tan-tien,* it will be difficult for you to lose your balance.

---

[1]This "chi" means breath and must not be confused with the "chi" of Tai-Chi Chuan.

# The Concept of *Din-Jin*

These two nouns, although they sound different, are the same in explanation and requirements.

*Din-jin* means that it seems as if there were a strong power wanting to ascend, but really there is no power at all; it is completely a function of the mind. The ancestors have said: "Mind concentrated on the head." The mind has no shape and is indefinite, and is therefore also called *shi-lin Din-jin*. *Shi-lin* means relaxed, flexible. *Din-jin* means to keep the head straight.

Two images may be useful for understanding *Din-jin:* 1) imagine that the head is held by a string, or 2) imagine that there is something on the head and it must be prevented from falling off. In both of these images, the head does not move forward or backward, nor from side to side. (However, the head does turn to the right or left in certain Tai-Chi Chuan movements. The key is to keep the head erect as you turn it.) Since the head is the most important portion of the human body, it must be held straight; only then are the poise and agility of the rest of the body sustained. By not holding the head properly, one easily loses one's balance and can be manipulated by others. The new learner cannot always do this well and very quickly gets a stiff neck. This comes from paying too much attention to the head. It is really very difficult for the beginner to learn to be aware and alert without thinking.

# IV

# INSTRUCTIONS
# FOR PUSHING HANDS

## Pushing Hands (Tui-Shou)

Pushing hands is an advanced exercise for learning the nature of force and developing sensitivity to changes in force by direct contact with a partner (called "opponent").[1] In pushing hands, one learns to distinguish between lightness and heaviness (*hsu* and *shih*), to recognize the origin of the opponent's force, and to sense when and what type of attack is imminent. The goal is to utilize the opponent's force rather than one's own for the counter-attack. When one is able to respond to the opponent so as to gain command of any situation, one has attained a true understanding of force — not just in the mind but in the body, and so, potentially, in the action of life.

---

[1]Rather than "partner" we use the term "opponent," as is traditional in the martial arts, although the goal of pushing hands as taught here is relationship rather than conflict.

## Technique for Basic One-Handed Method

Two persons stand facing one another. Each takes a step forward with the left foot, so that the toe of each one's left foot is placed at the opponent's left-foot arch. The rear, right foot is turned out, diagonally. The back of the right wrist is placed against the back of the opponent's right wrist. The left hand is held in a fist one inch in front of the center of the chest for protection (it's called the watch-dog). The two opponents begin pushing their right hands back and forth in a piston-like motion, describing an elongated oval, counter-clockwise. Each tries to push straight through the center of the other's chest, while protecting his own. (See pictures on the following page.) In order to deflect the opponent's thrusts, one must be flexible, twisting at the waist. Throughout the exercise, one tries to maintain the spine erect and torso relaxed, with the shoulders lined up over the hips.[2]

The exercise is then performed on the other side; substitute right for left and vice versa in the foregoing description, and describe the oval clockwise. The two may continue to switch from side to side, until they tire.

---

[2]This means that before beginning a movement, particularly an advance, on should be both internally and externally balanced. Externally, the center of gravity must be situated in the middle of the body. Internally, the intrinsic energy is composed and centered, so that when one moves, the energy neither jumps ahead nor lags behind the external movement. This might be thought of as not moving before you move.

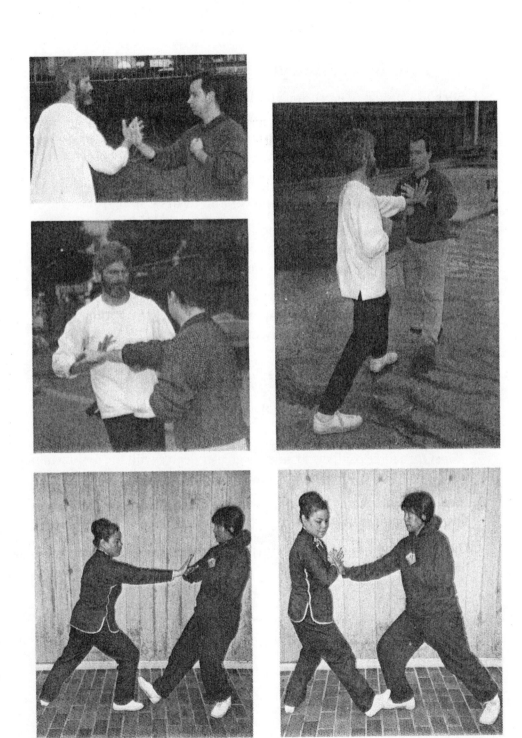

# Four Basic Strategies for Pushing Hands

1. **Stick to Upward** *(Chan):* Stick to the opponent and raise him up when pushing to uproot his center of gravity. Hands and arms are generally employed for Chan, but other parts of the body may be used in some situations.

2. **Attach** *(Tieh):* When engaging the opponent in struggle, attach yourself to his movements so as to prevent him from escaping you.

3. **Join** *(Lien):* Join with your opponent carefully in his every move. Let him take the lead, but never lose contact. In this way, tire the opponent out and cause him to expose his weak points.

4. **Follow Up** *(Sui):* Follow your opponent's movements and the direction of his force, watching for the opportunity to attack. Stay still if he does not move. Advance if he retreats, etc.

# Four Basic Mistakes

1. *Deen:* One unnecessarily resists the opponent's manifestations of force; thereby precious energy is wasted.

2. *Kan:* One's force conflicts to an even greater degree with the opponent's, until one is finally drawn into actively fighting his force.

3. *Pien:* One's movements are not properly timed (being too fast or too slow), so that it is impossible to adhere continuously to the opponent.

4. *Diu:* Not only is one's action ill-timed, but one loses all contact with the opponent's hand and arm.

# Eight Specific Techniques

1. **Ward Off Slanting Upward** *(Pung):* When the opponent pushes your forearm up in order to strike at your face, deflect the blow in an upward arc to the outside (to the right with the right hand, to the left with the left).

2. **Pull Back** *(Lee):* Using one hand to hold the opponent's wrist, place the other forearm against his arm and pull back (past his right side if pulling his right arm, and so on).

3. **Press Forward** *(Chi):* Use one hand to hold the opponent's wrist and place your other forearm against his upper arm to throw him back.

4. **Push** *(An):* When the opponent attacks you with his shoulder, step forward, place one foot between his legs, and push his forearm down with both hands.

5. **Pull Down** *(Tsai):* Holding the opponent's wrist with one hand, place the other hand on his wrist and pull him downward.

6. **Splitting** *(Lieh):* Grasp the opponent's wrist and quickly step forward so that the front foot is positioned behind him. Push through his chest so that he falls back over your leg.

7. **Elbow Stroke** *(Tso):* When the opponent holds your wrist and pulls you, use your other hand to grasp his wrist and free yours. The free arm is then bent to strike at the center of his chest with your elbow.

8. **Shoulder Stroke** *(Kow):* When the opponent pulls you, strike at the center of his chest with your shoulder. This move is difficult to apply, since it is ineffective if you are too close or too far away. The body must be centered, with one foot between the opponent's legs.[3]

---

[3]Using the intrinsic energy and the momentum of the waist and legs (as always), throw the shoulder forward. The intrinsic energy employed in this movement is called "inch energy" or "one-tenth-of-an-inch energy."

# Conclusion

To master pushing hands, and so to gain a deep understanding of force, requires long practice of the basic one-handed technique, standing in place, shifting occasionally from one side to the other. Only then should you try the advanced and unrestricted forms of pushing hands, where you move around quickly or slowly at will. These unrestricted forms are characterized by spontaneous movement in all directions. You follow your opponent without a break in the smooth flow of motion — whether advancing or retreating, turning, or changing positions.

Cat and dog pushing hands
(Mimi and Ling-Ling)

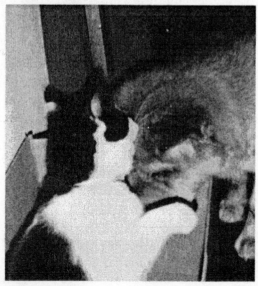

草木不經霜雪，
則生意不固。
吾心不經憂患，
則德慧不成。

*If the Grass and Trees Do Not Face*
*The Challenges of Frost and Snow,*
*Their Nature Will Not Be Strong.*
*If I Do Not Face Trials and Tribulations,*
*Virtuous Knowledge Cannot Be Attained.*

This is a photograph of my father as a young man. When our family was in great hunger many years ago, he refused to sell his only daughter. My father taught me that poverty is not embarrassing, but that greed is shameful. He died in 1972 at the age of 60.

This is my mother, now a Buddhist nun, whose example of patience and perseverance has helped me to complete this book.

# V

# · YU CHOU CHUNG (UNIVERSAL STANCE OR THE POST OF LIFE)

The Universal Stance position helps you gather strength through the development of mental concentration in a motionless exercise. Technique: This exercise requires you to stand upright and not bend towards one side or the other. Support yourself on one leg without tightening your muscles or bending that leg. Put the other leg forward and let it serve as a point of balance. Raise your arms forward and spread them to form a ring at shoulder height, as if you were embracing someone.[1] Breathe freely and naturally; look forward. Imagine that you are standing on a high mountaintop overlooking the ocean, and let your mental vision concentrate on looking out towards the horizon, across the water. Then, allow all the muscles throughout your body to relax (which also permits the blood to flow freely) so that you feel the *chi* sinking to the *tan-tien*. Stop whenever you begin to feel strain in your arms or tension in your shoulders. Do not force yourself beyond what feels good.

The aim of this exercise is to gather strength without making a physical effort, by concentrating all thought on activating the chi which nourishes strength. Thus, the main emphasis is on the development of the will. This outwardly motionless exercise requires no physical exertion and needs no muscular development. When you do this exercise, you must concentrate and think only about what you are doing. Forget about everything else, as this mental training stimulates body functions and activates the fine veins inside the large muscles. Thus the Universal Stance renews your energy and vitality.

For the cultivation of mental health, an effort should be made to achieve peace of mind while doing this silent exercise. Success comes from the relax-

---

[1] If the right foot is forward, the right hand is out a little bit farther than the left. See picture. If left foot is forward, the left hand is out farther.

ation of the body, the relaxation of the mind, the relaxation of the *chi*, and the freedom of the soul. Mental strength is the core of this exercise. Eventually, you feel that the whole universe is at your fingertips and that you are standing in the center of the world.

Therefore, the Universal Stance provides you with an opportunity to develop concentration, patience, and perseverance, but success will come only over a long period of time. Do not be impatient; never give up half-way through. Do the exercise every morning in the early hours (before sunrise) when the air is freshest. With sincere effort and practice, with diligence and determination, you will ultimately reap physical, mental, and spiritual benefits, but only if you have faith in the rewards of the Universal Stance.

# INTERNAL SYSTEM (EXERCISE) 內功
## YU CHOU CHUANG UNIVERSAL POST STANCE
## 宇宙樁

Fist, and yet, not a fist.
Meaning, and yet, no meaning;
Within the midst of meaninglessness is the true meaning.
To speak of truth is to be intelligent of no truth;
To cultivate the Way is to leave the body of toil.
　　From Classic of Tai-Chi Chuan by
　　Sifu Kuo Lien-Ying　郭連蔭

While these exercises can be very helpful to people who have had strokes or are debilitated in any way, it is essential to be supervised while doing them, because a certain risk may be involved. Do not do any of the exercises for more than a few minutes, or beyond the point of tiredness.

學而不思則罔．
思而不學則殆。
四書論語八十三頁

*Learning Without Thought Is Lost Labor:*
*Thought Without Learning Is Perilous.*

English Translation by James Legge

# 連蔭太極拳學院
## LIEN-YING TAI-CHI CHUAN ACADEMY

*The sharp point of the treasure sword*
*was honed on the grinding stone*

*The fragrance of the plum blossoms*
*was conceived in bitter cold*